55 Australian Recipes for Home

By: Kelly Johnson

Table of Contents

Appetizers and Starters:

- Prawn Cocktail
- Kangaroo Skewers with Bush Tomato Chutney
- Lamingtons (Sponge Cake Squares coated in Chocolate and Coconut)
- Smashed Avo Toast with Vegemite
- Australian Meat Pies
- Barramundi Ceviche with Finger Lime
- Damper (Traditional Australian Bush Bread)

Main Courses:

- Grilled Barramundi with Macadamia Pesto
- Kangaroo Steak with Red Wine Jus
- Salt and Pepper Calamari
- Chicken Parmigiana
- Vegemite and Cheese Scrolls
- Barramundi Fish and Chips
- Crocodile Skewers with Lemon Myrtle Marinade
- Australian Lamb Roast with Rosemary and Garlic
- Pumpkin and Fetta Risotto
- Butter Chicken Meat Pie
- Barramundi Burgers with Beetroot and Pineapple

BBQ and Grilling:

- Grilled Yabbies with Bush Tomato Butter
- BBQ Vegemite Chicken Wings
- Kangaroo Sausages with Bush Tomato Relish
- Grilled Moreton Bay Bugs with Garlic Butter
- BBQ Lamb Chops with Mint Sauce
- Vegemite-Marinated Shrimp Skewers
- BBQ Kangaroo Kebabs with Lemon Myrtle

Salads and Sides:

- Aussie Potato Salad
- Grilled Asparagus with Lemon Myrtle Butter
- Rocket and Parmesan Salad with Macadamia Dressing
- Coleslaw with Australian Granny Smith Apples
- Bush Tomato and Quinoa Salad
- Roasted Pumpkin and Chickpea Salad
- Tomato and Burrata Salad with Australian Olive Oil

Dips and Spreads:

- Macadamia and Bush Tomato Pesto
- Beetroot and Horseradish Dip
- Avocado and Vegemite Dip
- Lemon Myrtle Hummus
- Australian Bush Salsa with Native Herbs

Pasta and Noodles:

- Pumpkin Gnocchi with Sage Butter
- Crab Linguine with Finger Lime
- Spaghetti Carbonara with Australian Bacon

Desserts:

- Pavlova with Fresh Berries
- Lamington Ice Cream Sandwiches
- Wattleseed Chocolate Brownies
- Anzac Biscuits
- Macadamia Nut Brittle
- Tim Tam Cheesecake
- Lemon Myrtle and Honey Panna Cotta

Drinks:

- Australian Iced Coffee
- Eucalyptus and Mint Lemonade
- Kangaroo Island Gin and Tonic
- Bush Tucker Mojito
- Golden Gaytime Cocktail

Baking and Sweet Treats:

- Vanilla Slice
- Passionfruit Sponge Cake
- Milo Cheesecake

Appetizers and Starters:

Prawn Cocktail

Ingredients:

For the Cocktail Sauce:

- 1 cup mayonnaise
- 2 tablespoons ketchup
- 1 tablespoon lemon juice
- 1 teaspoon Worcestershire sauce
- 1 teaspoon hot sauce (adjust to taste)
- Salt and pepper to taste

For the Prawn Cocktail:

- 1 pound (about 450g) cooked and peeled prawns (shrimp), chilled
- 1 cup iceberg lettuce, shredded
- 1 avocado, diced
- 1 cucumber, diced
- Lemon wedges for garnish
- Fresh parsley for garnish

Instructions:

Cocktail Sauce:

    Prepare Sauce:
- In a bowl, whisk together mayonnaise, ketchup, lemon juice, Worcestershire sauce, hot sauce, salt, and pepper. Adjust the seasoning to your taste.

Prawn Cocktail:

    Prepare Prawns:
- Ensure the prawns are cooked, peeled, and chilled.

    Assemble Salad:
- In a large bowl, combine the shredded iceberg lettuce, diced avocado, and diced cucumber.

    Add Prawns:
- Gently fold in the cooked and peeled prawns.

    Coat with Sauce:

- Pour the cocktail sauce over the prawn mixture. Toss gently until everything is evenly coated with the sauce.

Chill:
- Place the prawn cocktail in the refrigerator to chill for at least 30 minutes.

Serve:
- Spoon the chilled prawn cocktail into serving glasses or bowls.

Garnish:
- Garnish with lemon wedges and fresh parsley.

Serve Cold:
- Serve the prawn cocktail cold as a refreshing appetizer or light meal.

Prawn Cocktail is a classic appetizer known for its combination of succulent prawns and a tangy cocktail sauce. It's elegant, easy to prepare, and perfect for serving at gatherings or as a starter for a special meal. Enjoy the delightful flavors of this timeless dish!

Kangaroo Skewers with Bush Tomato Chutney

Ingredients:

For Kangaroo Skewers:

- 1 pound (about 450g) kangaroo meat, diced into chunks
- 2 tablespoons olive oil
- 2 cloves garlic, minced
- 1 teaspoon ground cumin
- 1 teaspoon ground coriander
- Salt and black pepper to taste
- Wooden skewers, soaked in water

For Bush Tomato Chutney:

- 1 cup bush tomatoes, chopped
- 1 red onion, finely diced
- 2 tablespoons apple cider vinegar
- 2 tablespoons brown sugar
- 1 teaspoon ground ginger
- 1 teaspoon ground cinnamon
- Salt to taste

Instructions:

For Kangaroo Skewers:

Marinate Kangaroo Meat:
- In a bowl, combine olive oil, minced garlic, ground cumin, ground coriander, salt, and black pepper. Add the diced kangaroo meat to the marinade, ensuring it's well coated. Let it marinate for at least 30 minutes.

Skewer the Meat:
- Thread the marinated kangaroo meat onto the soaked wooden skewers.

Grill or Cook:
- Grill the skewers on a barbecue or cook them in a grill pan over medium-high heat until the kangaroo meat is cooked to your liking. Kangaroo meat is lean and cooks quickly, so be cautious not to overcook it.

For Bush Tomato Chutney:

Prepare Chutney Base:
- In a saucepan, combine chopped bush tomatoes, finely diced red onion, apple cider vinegar, brown sugar, ground ginger, ground cinnamon, and salt.

Cook Chutney:
- Cook the chutney over medium heat, stirring occasionally, until the tomatoes break down, and the mixture thickens. This may take about 15-20 minutes.

Adjust Seasoning:
- Taste the chutney and adjust the seasoning or sweetness according to your preference. Allow it to cool.

Serving:

Serve Skewers with Chutney:
- Arrange the kangaroo skewers on a serving platter. Serve them with a side of the bush tomato chutney.

Garnish (Optional):
- Garnish with fresh herbs, such as parsley or coriander, for added freshness.

Enjoy:
- Enjoy the unique and flavorful Kangaroo Skewers with Bush Tomato Chutney. They make for a distinctive and delicious dish with Australian flair.

Note: Kangaroo meat has a strong flavor and is best served medium-rare to medium. Adjust cooking times based on your preference for doneness.

Lamingtons (Sponge Cake Squares coated in Chocolate and Coconut)

Ingredients:

For the Sponge Cake:

- 1 cup (225g) unsalted butter, softened
- 1 cup (200g) granulated sugar
- 4 large eggs
- 1 teaspoon vanilla extract
- 2 cups (250g) all-purpose flour
- 2 teaspoons baking powder
- 1/2 cup (120ml) milk

For the Chocolate Icing:

- 3 cups (360g) powdered sugar
- 1/4 cup (25g) cocoa powder
- 1 tablespoon unsalted butter, melted
- 1/2 cup (120ml) milk
- Shredded coconut for coating

Instructions:

For the Sponge Cake:

Preheat Oven:
- Preheat your oven to 350°F (180°C). Grease and line a square baking pan (approximately 9x9 inches or 23x23 cm).

Cream Butter and Sugar:
- In a large bowl, cream together the softened butter and granulated sugar until light and fluffy.

Add Eggs and Vanilla:
- Add the eggs one at a time, beating well after each addition. Stir in the vanilla extract.

Combine Dry Ingredients:
- In a separate bowl, sift together the all-purpose flour and baking powder.

Alternate Adding Ingredients:
- Gradually add the sifted dry ingredients to the butter mixture, alternating with the milk. Begin and end with the dry ingredients. Mix until just combined.

Bake:
- Pour the batter into the prepared baking pan and smooth the top. Bake in the preheated oven for about 25-30 minutes or until a toothpick inserted into the center comes out clean.

Cool:
- Allow the sponge cake to cool completely in the pan before removing and cutting into squares.

For the Chocolate Icing:

Prepare Chocolate Icing:
- In a bowl, whisk together powdered sugar, cocoa powder, melted butter, and milk until smooth.

Coat Cake Squares:
- Dip each sponge cake square into the chocolate icing, ensuring it is well coated.

Coat with Shredded Coconut:
- Immediately roll the chocolate-coated square in shredded coconut, covering all sides. Place the coated Lamington on a wire rack to set.

Repeat:
- Repeat the process for each sponge cake square.

Let Set:
- Allow the Lamingtons to set completely before serving.

Serve:
- Serve the Lamingtons and enjoy these classic Australian treats!

Lamingtons are a beloved Australian dessert, and their light sponge cake squares coated in chocolate icing and shredded coconut make for a delightful and iconic sweet treat.

Smashed Avo Toast with Vegemite

Ingredients:

- 2 ripe avocados
- 1 tablespoon lemon juice
- Salt and black pepper to taste
- 4 slices of your favorite bread, toasted
- Vegemite (to taste)
- Optional toppings: cherry tomatoes, feta cheese, radishes, or microgreens

Instructions:

Smash Avocado:
- In a bowl, scoop out the flesh of the ripe avocados. Add lemon juice, salt, and black pepper. Use a fork to smash the avocados until you achieve your desired level of creaminess.

Toast Bread:
- Toast the slices of bread until golden brown and crispy.

Spread Vegemite:
- Spread Vegemite generously on each slice of toasted bread. Adjust the amount according to your taste preference.

Spread Smashed Avocado:
- Spoon the smashed avocado over the Vegemite-covered toast, spreading it evenly.

Add Optional Toppings:
- If desired, add toppings like halved cherry tomatoes, crumbled feta cheese, sliced radishes, or a sprinkle of microgreens.

Season:
- Optionally, add a dash of extra black pepper or a squeeze of lemon juice for additional flavor.

Serve:
- Serve the Smashed Avo Toast with Vegemite immediately for a delicious and satisfying breakfast or snack.

Smashed Avo Toast with Vegemite is a classic Australian breakfast or brunch option, combining the creamy texture of smashed avocado with the savory and distinct flavor of Vegemite. Feel free to customize it with your favorite toppings for a tasty and nutritious meal.

Australian Meat Pies

Ingredients:

For the Filling:

- 1 lb (450g) ground beef or a mix of beef and lamb
- 1 onion, finely chopped
- 2 cloves garlic, minced
- 1 carrot, grated
- 1 tablespoon tomato paste
- 2 tablespoons Worcestershire sauce
- 1 cup beef broth
- 2 tablespoons all-purpose flour
- Salt and pepper to taste
- Cooking oil

For the Pastry:

- 2 1/2 cups (320g) all-purpose flour
- 1 cup (225g) unsalted butter, cold and diced
- 1/2 cup (120ml) cold water
- Pinch of salt

For Assembly:

- Beaten egg for egg wash

Instructions:

For the Filling:

> Cook Vegetables:
> - In a large pan, heat oil over medium heat. Add chopped onions and cook until softened. Add minced garlic and grated carrot. Cook for a few minutes until the vegetables are tender.
>
> Add Meat:
> - Add ground beef (or beef and lamb mix) to the pan. Cook until browned, breaking it up with a spoon.
>
> Add Tomato Paste and Flour:

- Stir in tomato paste and flour, cooking for a couple of minutes to remove the raw taste of the flour.

Pour Broth and Worcestershire Sauce:
- Pour in beef broth and Worcestershire sauce. Stir well and let it simmer until the mixture thickens. Season with salt and pepper to taste.

Simmer:
- Simmer for about 15-20 minutes until the filling is thick and flavorful. Allow it to cool.

For the Pastry:

Prepare Pastry:
- In a large bowl, combine cold, diced butter with flour. Use your fingers or a pastry cutter to rub the butter into the flour until it resembles breadcrumbs.

Add Cold Water:
- Gradually add cold water, mixing until the dough comes together. Form it into a ball, cover with plastic wrap, and refrigerate for at least 30 minutes.

Preheat Oven:
- Preheat your oven to 400°F (200°C).

For Assembly:

Roll Out Pastry:
- Roll out the pastry on a floured surface to about 1/8 inch thickness. Cut circles large enough to fit into your pie molds.

Fill the Molds:
- Line pie molds with pastry, leaving some overhang. Fill each with the meat filling.

Top with Pastry:
- Place another pastry circle on top and crimp the edges to seal. Trim any excess pastry.

Brush with Egg Wash:
- Brush the tops with beaten egg for a golden finish.

Bake:
- Bake in the preheated oven for 20-25 minutes or until the pastry is golden brown and crisp.

Serve:
- Allow the Australian Meat Pies to cool slightly before serving. They can be enjoyed hot or at room temperature.

Australian Meat Pies are a beloved classic, often enjoyed at football games or as a quick and satisfying meal. The combination of flaky pastry and flavorful meat filling makes them a delicious treat for any occasion.

Barramundi Ceviche with Finger Lime

Ingredients:

- 1 lb (450g) barramundi fillets, skinless and boneless, diced into small cubes
- 1 cup finger lime pearls
- 1 red onion, finely diced
- 1 red chili, finely chopped
- 1/2 cup fresh cilantro, chopped
- 1/2 cup fresh mint, chopped
- Juice of 5-6 limes
- Juice of 1 lemon
- Salt and pepper to taste
- 2 tablespoons olive oil
- Tostadas or tortilla chips for serving

Instructions:

Prepare Barramundi:
- Ensure the barramundi fillets are fresh, skinless, and boneless. Dice them into small, bite-sized cubes.

Combine Ingredients:
- In a large bowl, combine the diced barramundi, finger lime pearls, finely diced red onion, chopped red chili, fresh cilantro, and fresh mint.

Add Citrus Juices:
- Squeeze the juice of limes and lemon over the ingredients. Ensure the fish is well-coated in the citrus juices.

Season:
- Season the ceviche with salt and pepper to taste. Adjust the seasoning as needed.

Marinate:
- Allow the barramundi ceviche to marinate in the citrus juices for about 15-20 minutes. The acid from the citrus will "cook" the fish, giving it a ceviche texture.

Add Olive Oil:
- Drizzle olive oil over the ceviche and gently toss to combine. The olive oil adds richness to the dish.

Chill:
- Refrigerate the barramundi ceviche for an additional 15-20 minutes to enhance the flavors and ensure it's well-chilled.

Serve:
- Spoon the barramundi ceviche onto tostadas or serve with tortilla chips.

Garnish:
- Garnish with additional cilantro or mint leaves for freshness.

Enjoy:
- Serve the Barramundi Ceviche with Finger Lime immediately and enjoy the vibrant flavors of this refreshing dish.

Barramundi Ceviche with Finger Lime is a delightful and elegant appetizer, showcasing the freshness of barramundi fish and the unique burst of flavor from finger limes. It's perfect for a light and refreshing start to any meal.

Damper (Traditional Australian Bush Bread)

Ingredients:

For the Crust:
- 2 cups chocolate cookie crumbs
- 1/2 cup unsalted butter, melted

For the Cheesecake Filling:
- 24 oz (680g) cream cheese, softened
- 1 cup granulated sugar
- 3/4 cup Milo powder
- 4 large eggs
- 1 teaspoon vanilla extract
- 1/2 cup sour cream

For the Topping:
- 1 cup whipped cream
- Additional Milo powder for dusting

Instructions:

For the Crust:

Preheat Oven:
- Preheat your oven to 325°F (160°C). Grease a 9-inch springform pan.

Combine Crumbs and Butter:
- In a bowl, mix the chocolate cookie crumbs and melted butter until well combined.

Press into Pan:
- Press the mixture into the bottom of the prepared springform pan to create an even crust.

Bake:
- Bake the crust in the preheated oven for about 10 minutes. Remove and let it cool while you prepare the cheesecake filling.

For the Cheesecake Filling:

Reduce Oven Temperature:
- Reduce the oven temperature to 300°F (150°C).

Prepare Cream Cheese Mixture:
- In a large bowl, beat the softened cream cheese until smooth. Add sugar and Milo powder, continuing to beat until well combined.

Add Eggs:
- Add the eggs one at a time, mixing well after each addition.

Incorporate Vanilla and Sour Cream:
- Mix in the vanilla extract and sour cream until the mixture is smooth.

Pour into Crust:
- Pour the cream cheese mixture over the prepared crust in the springform pan.

Bake:
- Bake in the preheated oven for about 50-60 minutes or until the center is set. The edges should be slightly golden.

Cool and Chill:
- Allow the cheesecake to cool in the pan, then refrigerate for several hours or overnight.

For the Topping:
- Whip Cream:
  - Whip the cream until stiff peaks form.
- Top Cheesecake:
  - Spread the whipped cream over the chilled cheesecake.

- Dust with Milo:
    - Dust the top of the cheesecake with additional Milo powder.
- Slice and Serve:
    - Slice and serve this decadent Milo Cheesecake. Enjoy the rich chocolatey flavor and creamy texture!
- Note:
    - You can also drizzle chocolate syrup or ganache over the top for an extra chocolatey touch if desired.

- 4 cups (500g) self-rising flour
- Pinch of salt
- 1 cup (250ml) milk
- 1/2 cup (125ml) water (adjust as needed)
- Butter or golden syrup for serving

Instructions:

Preheat Oven:
- Preheat your oven to 400°F (200°C). Dust a baking sheet with flour or line it with parchment paper.

Combine Dry Ingredients:
- In a large mixing bowl, combine the self-rising flour and a pinch of salt.

Add Wet Ingredients:
- Make a well in the center of the flour mixture and pour in the milk. Gradually add water while mixing until a soft dough forms.

Knead Dough:
- Turn the dough onto a floured surface and knead it lightly until it comes together. Avoid over-kneading, as damper is meant to be a rustic and hearty bread.

Shape Damper:
- Shape the dough into a round loaf, approximately 1.5 to 2 inches thick.

Score the Top:
- Use a sharp knife to score a deep cross into the top of the damper. This helps the bread cook evenly.

Bake:

- Place the shaped damper on the prepared baking sheet. Bake in the preheated oven for about 30-40 minutes or until the damper sounds hollow when tapped on the bottom.

Cool:
- Allow the damper to cool on a wire rack.

Serve:
- Slice the damper and serve it warm with butter or golden syrup.

Enjoy:
- Enjoy this traditional Australian bush bread with your favorite toppings or as a side to soups and stews.

Damper is a classic Australian bread with a history rooted in the bush. It's easy to make and perfect for sharing around a campfire or enjoying as a simple, rustic bread at home. The dense texture and hearty flavor make it a favorite among Australians.

Main Courses:

Grilled Barramundi with Macadamia Pesto

Ingredients:

For Barramundi:

- 4 barramundi fillets
- Salt and black pepper to taste
- Olive oil for brushing

For Macadamia Pesto:

- 1 cup roasted macadamia nuts
- 2 cups fresh basil leaves
- 1/2 cup grated Parmesan cheese
- 2 cloves garlic, peeled
- 1/2 cup extra-virgin olive oil
- Salt and black pepper to taste
- Lemon wedges for serving

Instructions:

For Macadamia Pesto:

  Prepare Macadamia Nuts:
  - If the macadamia nuts are not already roasted, roast them in a dry pan over medium heat until they are golden and fragrant. Allow them to cool.

  Blend Ingredients:
  - In a food processor, combine roasted macadamia nuts, fresh basil leaves, grated Parmesan cheese, and peeled garlic cloves. Pulse until coarsely chopped.

  Add Olive Oil:
  - With the food processor running, gradually pour in the extra-virgin olive oil until the mixture reaches a smooth consistency.

  Season:
  - Season the pesto with salt and black pepper to taste. Adjust the seasoning if necessary.

For Grilled Barramundi:

  Preheat Grill:

- Preheat the grill to medium-high heat.

Season Barramundi:
- Season the barramundi fillets with salt and black pepper.

Brush with Olive Oil:
- Brush the barramundi fillets with olive oil to prevent sticking to the grill.

Grill:
- Place the barramundi fillets on the preheated grill. Grill for about 4-6 minutes per side or until the fish is cooked through and has grill marks.

Serve:
- Transfer the grilled barramundi to serving plates. Spoon macadamia pesto over the fillets.

Garnish:
- Garnish with additional fresh basil leaves and serve with lemon wedges on the side.

Enjoy:
- Serve the Grilled Barramundi with Macadamia Pesto immediately, and enjoy the delicious combination of flavors.

Grilled Barramundi with Macadamia Pesto is a flavorful and elegant dish that showcases the unique taste of barramundi complemented by the richness of macadamia pesto. It's a perfect choice for a special meal or when you want to impress with a delightful seafood dish.

Kangaroo Steak with Red Wine Jus

Ingredients:

For Kangaroo Steak:

- 4 kangaroo steaks (about 6 oz each)
- Salt and black pepper to taste
- 2 tablespoons olive oil
- 2 cloves garlic, minced
- 2 sprigs of fresh rosemary

For Red Wine Jus:

- 1 cup red wine
- 1 cup beef stock
- 1 shallot, finely chopped
- 2 tablespoons unsalted butter
- Salt and black pepper to taste

Instructions:

For Kangaroo Steak:

Preheat Grill:
- Preheat your grill to medium-high heat.

Season Kangaroo Steaks:
- Season the kangaroo steaks with salt and black pepper. Rub olive oil over the steaks, and sprinkle minced garlic on both sides. Place fresh rosemary sprigs on top.

Grill Kangaroo Steaks:
- Grill the kangaroo steaks for about 3-4 minutes on each side for medium-rare, or adjust the cooking time according to your preference.

Rest:
- Remove the steaks from the grill and let them rest for a few minutes before serving.

For Red Wine Jus:

Prepare Red Wine Jus:
- While the kangaroo steaks are resting, prepare the red wine jus. In a saucepan, combine red wine, beef stock, and chopped shallot. Bring it to a simmer over medium heat.

Reduce and Strain:
- Allow the mixture to reduce by half, stirring occasionally. Once reduced, strain the liquid to remove the shallot.

Finish with Butter:
- Return the strained liquid to the saucepan and whisk in unsalted butter. Simmer for a few more minutes until the sauce thickens slightly.

Season:
- Season the red wine jus with salt and black pepper to taste.

Serving:

Plate Kangaroo Steaks:
- Place the grilled kangaroo steaks on serving plates.

Drizzle with Red Wine Jus:
- Drizzle the red wine jus over the kangaroo steaks.

Serve:
- Serve the Kangaroo Steak with Red Wine Jus immediately, accompanied by your favorite sides.

This Kangaroo Steak with Red Wine Jus is a sophisticated and flavorful dish, showcasing the unique taste of kangaroo meat. The red wine jus adds a rich and velvety finish to the grilled steaks, making it a delightful main course for special occasions.

Salt and Pepper Calamari

Ingredients:

- 1 lb (450g) fresh calamari tubes, cleaned and sliced into rings
- 1 cup buttermilk
- 1 cup all-purpose flour
- 1 teaspoon salt
- 1 teaspoon black pepper
- 1 teaspoon paprika
- Vegetable oil for frying
- Fresh lemon wedges for serving

Instructions:

Prepare Calamari:
- Clean the calamari tubes and slice them into rings. Pat them dry with paper towels.

Marinate in Buttermilk:
- Place the calamari rings in a bowl and pour buttermilk over them. Allow them to marinate for at least 30 minutes, or refrigerate for up to 4 hours for enhanced tenderness.

Prepare Coating Mixture:
- In a shallow dish, combine flour, salt, black pepper, and paprika. Mix well to create the seasoned coating.

Coat Calamari:
- Remove the calamari rings from the buttermilk, allowing any excess to drip off. Toss the rings in the seasoned flour mixture, ensuring each piece is well-coated.

Heat Oil:
- In a deep fryer or large, deep skillet, heat vegetable oil to 350°F (180°C).

Fry Calamari:
- Fry the coated calamari rings in batches for 1-2 minutes or until they are golden brown and crispy. Be careful not to overcrowd the fryer to ensure even cooking.

Drain and Season:
- Remove the fried calamari with a slotted spoon and place them on a plate lined with paper towels to drain any excess oil. Immediately season with additional salt and pepper if desired.

Serve:

- Serve the Salt and Pepper Calamari hot, garnished with fresh lemon wedges.

Optional:
- You can serve it with your favorite dipping sauces, such as aioli or marinara.

Enjoy:
- Enjoy the crispy and flavorful Salt and Pepper Calamari as a delicious appetizer or snack.

This Salt and Pepper Calamari recipe delivers perfectly crispy and seasoned calamari rings. It's a popular and delightful dish that makes for a fantastic appetizer or light meal. Serve it with a squeeze of fresh lemon for a burst of citrus flavor.

Chicken Parmigiana

Ingredients:

For Chicken:

- 4 boneless, skinless chicken breasts
- Salt and black pepper to taste
- 1 cup all-purpose flour
- 2 large eggs, beaten
- 1 cup breadcrumbs
- 1 cup grated Parmesan cheese
- 1 cup marinara sauce
- 1 cup shredded mozzarella cheese
- Olive oil for frying

For Garnish:

- Fresh basil or parsley, chopped
- Grated Parmesan cheese

Instructions:

Preheat Oven:
- Preheat your oven to 375°F (190°C).

Prepare Chicken:
- Season the chicken breasts with salt and black pepper.

Coating Station:
- Set up a coating station with three shallow bowls. Fill one with flour, another with beaten eggs, and the third with a mixture of breadcrumbs and grated Parmesan.

Coat Chicken:
- Dredge each chicken breast in the flour, dip into the beaten eggs, and then coat thoroughly with the breadcrumb and Parmesan mixture.

Fry Chicken:
- In a large skillet, heat olive oil over medium-high heat. Fry the coated chicken breasts until golden brown and cooked through, about 3-4 minutes per side. Place the cooked chicken on a paper towel-lined plate to absorb excess oil.

Assemble Parmigiana:

- In a baking dish, spread a thin layer of marinara sauce. Place the fried chicken breasts on top. Spoon more marinara sauce over each chicken breast.

Add Mozzarella:
- Sprinkle shredded mozzarella cheese over each chicken breast, ensuring they are well-covered.

Bake:
- Bake in the preheated oven for 20-25 minutes or until the cheese is melted and bubbly.

Broil (Optional):
- If desired, broil for an additional 1-2 minutes to achieve a golden brown top.

Garnish:
- Remove from the oven and garnish with chopped fresh basil or parsley and additional grated Parmesan cheese.

Serve:
- Serve the Chicken Parmigiana over a bed of pasta or with a side of salad. Enjoy!

Chicken Parmigiana, or Chicken Parmesan, is a classic Italian-American dish featuring breaded and fried chicken breasts topped with marinara sauce and melted mozzarella. It's a comforting and delicious meal that pairs well with pasta or a simple side salad.

Vegemite and Cheese Scrolls

Ingredients:

- 2 1/2 cups self-rising flour
- 1 cup grated cheddar cheese
- 1/4 cup butter, cold and diced
- 1 cup milk
- Vegemite, to spread
- Additional cheese for topping (optional)

Instructions:

Preheat Oven:
- Preheat your oven to 425°F (220°C). Grease or line a baking tray.

Prepare Dough:
- In a large mixing bowl, combine self-rising flour and grated cheddar cheese.

Add Butter:
- Add the cold, diced butter to the flour and cheese mixture. Use your fingers or a pastry cutter to rub the butter into the dry ingredients until the mixture resembles breadcrumbs.

Add Milk:
- Gradually add the milk, stirring with a wooden spoon until a soft dough forms.

Knead Dough:
- Turn the dough onto a floured surface and knead it lightly for a few minutes until it comes together.

Roll Out Dough:
- Roll out the dough into a rectangle, approximately 1/2 inch (1 cm) thick.

Spread Vegemite:
- Spread a layer of Vegemite over the rolled-out dough, covering it evenly.

Roll Up Dough:
- Starting from one of the longer edges, roll the dough into a log or cylinder.

Slice Scrolls:
- Using a sharp knife, slice the rolled-up dough into even-sized scrolls, about 1 inch (2.5 cm) thick.

Place on Baking Tray:
- Place the Vegemite and Cheese Scrolls on the prepared baking tray, leaving a little space between each scroll.

Optional Cheese Topping:
- If desired, sprinkle additional grated cheese on top of the scrolls.

Bake:
- Bake in the preheated oven for 12-15 minutes or until the scrolls are golden brown and cooked through.

Cool:
- Allow the scrolls to cool slightly on the tray before transferring them to a wire rack to cool completely.

Serve:
- Serve the Vegemite and Cheese Scrolls warm or at room temperature. Enjoy as a snack or light meal!

These Vegemite and Cheese Scrolls are a savory and delicious twist on the classic cinnamon scroll. The combination of Vegemite and cheese creates a uniquely Australian flavor that's perfect for breakfast, brunch, or as a tasty snack.

Barramundi Fish and Chips

Ingredients:

For Barramundi:

- 4 barramundi fillets
- 1 cup all-purpose flour
- 1 teaspoon garlic powder
- 1 teaspoon paprika
- Salt and black pepper to taste
- 2 eggs, beaten
- Vegetable oil for frying

For Chips (Fries):

- 4 large potatoes, peeled and cut into thick strips
- Vegetable oil for frying
- Salt to taste

For Tartar Sauce:

- 1 cup mayonnaise
- 2 tablespoons chopped pickles
- 1 tablespoon capers, chopped
- 1 tablespoon fresh parsley, chopped
- 1 tablespoon Dijon mustard
- 1 tablespoon lemon juice
- Salt and black pepper to taste

Instructions:

For Barramundi:

Preheat Oil:
- Heat vegetable oil in a deep fryer or large, deep skillet to 350°F (180°C).

Prepare Coating:
- In a shallow dish, combine flour, garlic powder, paprika, salt, and black pepper. Mix well.

Coat Barramundi:
- Dredge each barramundi fillet in the seasoned flour mixture, then dip it into beaten eggs, and again coat it with the flour mixture.

Fry Barramundi:
- Fry the coated barramundi fillets for 3-4 minutes per side or until they are golden brown and cooked through. Place them on a paper towel-lined plate to drain excess oil.

For Chips (Fries):

Preheat Oil for Chips:
- Heat vegetable oil in a separate fryer or pan to 350°F (180°C).

Fry Chips:
- Fry the potato strips in batches until they are golden brown and crispy. Remove them from the oil and drain on paper towels. Season with salt immediately.

For Tartar Sauce:

Prepare Tartar Sauce:
- In a bowl, mix together mayonnaise, chopped pickles, capers, fresh parsley, Dijon mustard, lemon juice, salt, and black pepper. Adjust the seasoning to taste.

Serving:

Serve:
- Serve the crispy Barramundi Fish alongside the golden Chips. Drizzle with fresh lemon juice and serve with a side of homemade Tartar Sauce.

Garnish (Optional):
- Garnish with additional fresh parsley or lemon wedges if desired.

Enjoy:
- Enjoy this classic Barramundi Fish and Chips recipe, a delicious and satisfying meal with a crisp exterior and tender barramundi inside.

Barramundi Fish and Chips is a popular and beloved dish that combines crispy fried fish with golden, perfectly cooked chips. It's a classic takeaway meal that you can easily recreate at home for a delightful and flavorful experience.

Crocodile Skewers with Lemon Myrtle Marinade

Ingredients:

For Crocodile Skewers:

- 1 lb (450g) crocodile tail meat, cut into bite-sized cubes
- Wooden skewers, soaked in water for 30 minutes

For Lemon Myrtle Marinade:

- 1/4 cup olive oil
- 2 tablespoons lemon myrtle leaves, finely chopped
- 2 cloves garlic, minced
- 1 tablespoon honey
- 1 tablespoon Dijon mustard
- 1 tablespoon lemon juice
- Salt and black pepper to taste

Instructions:

Prepare Crocodile Skewers:
- If using wooden skewers, soak them in water for at least 30 minutes to prevent burning during grilling. Cut the crocodile tail meat into bite-sized cubes.

Prepare Lemon Myrtle Marinade:
- In a bowl, whisk together olive oil, finely chopped lemon myrtle leaves, minced garlic, honey, Dijon mustard, lemon juice, salt, and black pepper. This will be your marinade.

Marinate Crocodile Meat:
- Place the crocodile cubes in a shallow dish or a zip-top bag. Pour the lemon myrtle marinade over the crocodile meat, ensuring each piece is well-coated. Marinate for at least 30 minutes, or refrigerate for up to 4 hours for enhanced flavor.

Skewer Crocodile Meat:
- Thread the marinated crocodile cubes onto the soaked wooden skewers.

Preheat Grill:
- Preheat your grill to medium-high heat.

Grill Skewers:
- Grill the crocodile skewers for about 3-4 minutes per side or until they are cooked through and have a nice char.

Baste with Marinade:
- During grilling, baste the skewers with additional lemon myrtle marinade to keep them moist and flavorful.

Serve:
- Once the crocodile skewers are cooked, remove them from the grill and let them rest for a few minutes.

Garnish (Optional):
- Garnish with fresh lemon myrtle leaves or a wedge of lemon for an extra burst of flavor.

Enjoy:
- Serve the Crocodile Skewers with Lemon Myrtle Marinade as a unique and flavorful appetizer or main dish. Enjoy the exotic taste of crocodile complemented by the aromatic lemon myrtle marinade.

Note: Ensure that the crocodile meat is sourced from a reputable supplier and properly prepared for consumption. Cooking times may vary, so monitor the skewers closely to prevent overcooking.

Australian Lamb Roast with Rosemary and Garlic

Ingredients:

- 1 leg of Australian lamb (about 5-6 lbs)
- 4 cloves garlic, minced
- 2 tablespoons fresh rosemary, finely chopped
- 2 tablespoons olive oil
- Salt and black pepper to taste
- 1 cup red wine (optional)
- 1 cup beef or vegetable broth
- 2 tablespoons all-purpose flour (for gravy)

Instructions:

Preheat Oven:
- Preheat your oven to 350°F (180°C).

Prepare Lamb:
- Place the leg of lamb on a cutting board. Using a sharp knife, make small incisions or slits all over the lamb.

Make Garlic-Rosemary Mixture:
- In a small bowl, mix minced garlic, chopped rosemary, olive oil, salt, and black pepper to create a paste.

Rub Lamb with Mixture:
- Rub the garlic-rosemary mixture all over the leg of lamb, ensuring it gets into the incisions for maximum flavor.

Optional: Wine Marinade (Skip if not using):
- If time allows, you can let the lamb marinate in red wine for a few hours in the refrigerator. This step is optional but adds depth of flavor.

Place in Roasting Pan:
- Place the lamb in a roasting pan, fat side up.

Roast:
- Roast the lamb in the preheated oven for about 20 minutes per pound, or until the internal temperature reaches your desired level of doneness. For medium-rare, aim for an internal temperature of 135°F (57°C), and for medium, aim for 145°F (63°C).

Baste:
- Baste the lamb with its juices every 20-30 minutes during roasting.

Rest:

- Once cooked to your liking, remove the lamb from the oven and let it rest for at least 15-20 minutes before carving.

Prepare Gravy:
- While the lamb is resting, make the gravy. Pour the pan juices into a saucepan. In a separate bowl, mix flour with a little water to create a smooth paste. Whisk the flour paste into the pan juices, add beef or vegetable broth, and cook over medium heat until the gravy thickens.

Carve and Serve:
- Carve the lamb into slices and serve it with the rosemary and garlic gravy.

Enjoy:
- Enjoy your Australian Lamb Roast with Rosemary and Garlic, a classic and flavorful dish that's perfect for special occasions or Sunday dinners.

Pumpkin and Fetta Risotto

Ingredients:

- 1 1/2 cups Arborio rice
- 1 cup pumpkin, diced into small cubes
- 1/2 cup crumbled feta cheese
- 1 onion, finely chopped
- 2 cloves garlic, minced
- 4 cups vegetable or chicken broth, kept warm
- 1/2 cup dry white wine
- 1/4 cup grated Parmesan cheese
- 2 tablespoons olive oil
- 1 tablespoon butter
- Salt and black pepper to taste
- Fresh parsley, chopped, for garnish

Instructions:

Prepare Pumpkin:
- Preheat your oven to 400°F (200°C). Toss the diced pumpkin in olive oil, salt, and pepper. Roast in the oven until tender and slightly caramelized, about 20-25 minutes.

Sauté Onions and Garlic:
- In a large, heavy-bottomed pan, heat olive oil over medium heat. Add chopped onions and cook until translucent. Add minced garlic and sauté for another 1-2 minutes.

Toast Arborio Rice:
- Add Arborio rice to the pan and stir to coat the rice with the oil. Toast the rice for 2-3 minutes until the edges become translucent.

Deglaze with Wine:
- Pour in the white wine and stir until it's mostly absorbed by the rice.

Add Broth:
- Begin adding the warm broth, one ladle at a time, stirring frequently. Allow each ladle of broth to be mostly absorbed before adding the next.

Continue Cooking:
- Continue this process until the rice is creamy and cooked to al dente. This will take about 18-20 minutes.

Incorporate Roasted Pumpkin:
- Once the rice is almost cooked, fold in the roasted pumpkin cubes.

Finish with Butter and Cheese:
- Stir in butter, grated Parmesan cheese, and crumbled feta cheese. Season with salt and black pepper to taste. Continue stirring until the cheeses are melted, and the risotto has a creamy consistency.

Adjust Consistency:
- If needed, add a little more warm broth or hot water to achieve your desired consistency.

Garnish and Serve:
- Garnish the Pumpkin and Feta Risotto with chopped fresh parsley. Serve immediately.

Enjoy:
- Enjoy this creamy and flavorful Pumpkin and Feta Risotto as a delicious and satisfying meal.

Butter Chicken Meat Pie

Ingredients:

For Butter Chicken Filling:

- 1 lb (450g) boneless, skinless chicken thighs, cut into bite-sized pieces
- 1 large onion, finely chopped
- 3 cloves garlic, minced
- 1 tablespoon ginger, grated
- 1/2 cup butter chicken sauce
- 1/2 cup tomato puree
- 1/2 cup heavy cream
- 1 teaspoon garam masala
- 1/2 teaspoon turmeric
- 1/2 teaspoon paprika
- Salt and black pepper to taste
- 2 tablespoons vegetable oil

For Pie Crust:

- 2 1/2 cups all-purpose flour
- 1 cup unsalted butter, cold and diced
- 1/2 cup ice water
- 1 teaspoon salt

Additional:

- 1 egg (for egg wash)
- Sesame seeds (optional, for garnish)

Instructions:

For Butter Chicken Filling:

Sauté Chicken:
- In a large skillet, heat vegetable oil over medium-high heat. Sauté chopped onions until translucent. Add minced garlic and grated ginger, and cook for another 1-2 minutes. Add chicken pieces and brown them on all sides.

Add Spices:

- Sprinkle garam masala, turmeric, paprika, salt, and black pepper over the chicken. Stir well to coat the chicken with the spices.

Combine Sauces:
- Pour in the butter chicken sauce, tomato puree, and heavy cream. Stir to combine, and let it simmer over medium heat until the chicken is cooked through and the sauce thickens.

Simmer:
- Simmer for an additional 10-15 minutes, allowing the flavors to meld. Adjust seasoning if needed.

For Pie Crust:

Prepare Pie Crust:
- In a food processor, combine all-purpose flour and diced cold butter. Pulse until the mixture resembles coarse crumbs. Add ice water and salt, and pulse until the dough comes together. Shape the dough into a disc, wrap it in plastic wrap, and refrigerate for at least 30 minutes.

Roll Out Dough:
- Preheat your oven to 375°F (190°C). Roll out the chilled pie crust on a floured surface to fit your pie dish.

Assemble Pie:
- Line the bottom of a pie dish with half of the rolled-out pie crust. Pour the butter chicken filling into the crust. Cover with the remaining pie crust. Trim any excess and crimp the edges to seal.

Egg Wash and Garnish:
- Beat an egg and brush it over the top crust for a golden finish. Optionally, sprinkle sesame seeds for garnish.

Bake:
- Bake in the preheated oven for 30-35 minutes or until the crust is golden brown.

Cool and Serve:
- Allow the Butter Chicken Meat Pie to cool for a few minutes before slicing and serving.

Enjoy:
- Enjoy this fusion twist on a classic meat pie with the rich and flavorful Butter Chicken filling. Serve it with a side of your favorite chutney or raita.

Barramundi Burgers with Beetroot and Pineapple

Ingredients:

For Barramundi Patties:

- 1 lb (450g) barramundi fillets, skinless and boneless
- 1/2 cup breadcrumbs
- 1/4 cup mayonnaise
- 1 tablespoon Dijon mustard
- 1 tablespoon lemon juice
- 2 green onions, finely chopped
- 1 teaspoon Old Bay seasoning (or seafood seasoning of choice)
- Salt and black pepper to taste
- 2 tablespoons vegetable oil (for cooking)

For Burgers:

- Burger buns
- Lettuce leaves
- Sliced beetroot (canned or cooked)
- Sliced pineapple rings (fresh or canned)
- Additional condiments of choice (mayonnaise, ketchup, etc.)

Instructions:

For Barramundi Patties:

Prepare Barramundi:
- Pat the barramundi fillets dry with paper towels. Cut them into chunks and place them in a food processor.

Make Patties:
- Pulse the barramundi in the food processor until it reaches a coarse texture. In a mixing bowl, combine the processed barramundi, breadcrumbs, mayonnaise, Dijon mustard, lemon juice, chopped green onions, Old Bay seasoning, salt, and black pepper. Mix well.

Form Patties:
- Divide the mixture into equal portions and shape them into patties. Place the patties on a plate lined with parchment paper.

Chill Patties:
- Refrigerate the barramundi patties for at least 30 minutes to help them firm up.

Cook Patties:

- Heat vegetable oil in a skillet over medium-high heat. Cook the barramundi patties for about 3-4 minutes per side or until they are golden brown and cooked through.

Assemble Burgers:

Prepare Burger Buns:
- Toast the burger buns lightly on a grill or in a toaster.

Assemble:
- Spread your preferred condiments on the bottom half of the bun. Place a barramundi patty on top.

Layer Ingredients:
- Add lettuce leaves, sliced beetroot, and a pineapple ring on each patty.

Top and Serve:
- Place the top half of the bun on the assembled ingredients. Secure the burger with a toothpick if needed.

Repeat:
- Repeat the process for the remaining barramundi patties.

Serve:
- Serve the Barramundi Burgers with Beetroot and Pineapple immediately, and enjoy this delightful combination of flavors.

These Barramundi Burgers with Beetroot and Pineapple offer a fresh and tropical twist on the classic burger. The barramundi patties bring a light and flaky texture, complemented by the sweetness of pineapple and earthiness of beetroot. Customize with your favorite condiments for a delicious and satisfying meal.

BBQ and Grilling:

Grilled Yabbies with Bush Tomato Butter

Ingredients:

For Grilled Yabbies:

- 1 lb (450g) fresh yabbies, cleaned and deveined
- 2 tablespoons olive oil
- Salt and black pepper to taste
- Lemon wedges for serving

For Bush Tomato Butter:

- 1/2 cup unsalted butter, softened
- 2 tablespoons bush tomato chutney or bush tomato relish
- 1 tablespoon fresh parsley, finely chopped
- 1 teaspoon lemon juice
- Salt and black pepper to taste

Instructions:

For Grilled Yabbies:

   Preheat Grill:
   - Preheat your grill to medium-high heat.

   Prepare Yabbies:
   - Rinse the yabbies under cold water. Pat them dry with paper towels.

   Season Yabbies:
   - In a bowl, toss the yabbies with olive oil, salt, and black pepper. Ensure they are evenly coated.

   Grill Yabbies:
   - Place the seasoned yabbies on the preheated grill. Grill for about 2-3 minutes per side or until they are opaque and cooked through. Be cautious not to overcook, as yabbies can become tough.

   Remove from Grill:
   - Once cooked, remove the grilled yabbies from the grill and set aside.

For Bush Tomato Butter:

Make Bush Tomato Butter:
- In a small bowl, combine softened butter, bush tomato chutney, chopped fresh parsley, lemon juice, salt, and black pepper. Mix well until all ingredients are incorporated.

Serve:
- Serve the grilled yabbies on a platter with lemon wedges. Spoon the bush tomato butter over the yabbies or serve it on the side as a dipping sauce.

Garnish (Optional):
- Garnish with additional fresh parsley for a burst of color.

Enjoy:
- Enjoy the Grilled Yabbies with Bush Tomato Butter as a flavorful and succulent seafood dish. The bush tomato butter adds a unique Australian twist to the classic grilled yabby experience.

BBQ Vegemite Chicken Wings

Ingredients:

For Chicken Wings:

- 2 lbs (about 1 kg) chicken wings, split at joints, tips discarded
- 2 tablespoons olive oil
- Salt and black pepper to taste

For BBQ Vegemite Glaze:

- 3 tablespoons Vegemite
- 2 tablespoons honey
- 1 tablespoon soy sauce
- 2 tablespoons tomato ketchup
- 1 teaspoon garlic powder
- 1 teaspoon onion powder
- 1 teaspoon smoked paprika
- 2 tablespoons olive oil
- Sesame seeds and chopped green onions for garnish (optional)

Instructions:

For Chicken Wings:

    Preheat Grill:
- Preheat your grill to medium-high heat.

    Prepare Chicken Wings:
- In a large bowl, toss the chicken wings with olive oil, salt, and black pepper until evenly coated.

    Grill Chicken Wings:
- Place the seasoned chicken wings on the preheated grill. Grill for about 20-25 minutes, turning occasionally, or until the wings are cooked through and have a nice char.

For BBQ Vegemite Glaze:

    Prepare Glaze:

- In a small saucepan over medium heat, combine Vegemite, honey, soy sauce, tomato ketchup, garlic powder, onion powder, smoked paprika, and olive oil. Stir until the mixture is well combined and heated through.

Glaze Chicken Wings:
- Brush the BBQ Vegemite glaze over the grilled chicken wings during the last 5 minutes of cooking. Make sure to coat the wings evenly on all sides.

Caramelization:
- Allow the glaze to caramelize slightly on the wings, creating a flavorful and sticky coating.

Garnish (Optional):
- Sprinkle sesame seeds and chopped green onions over the glazed wings for an extra touch of flavor and visual appeal.

Serve:
- Transfer the BBQ Vegemite Chicken Wings to a serving platter.

Enjoy:
- Serve immediately and enjoy these uniquely Australian BBQ Vegemite Chicken Wings as a delicious appetizer or main course. They are sure to be a hit at any barbecue or gathering.

Kangaroo Sausages with Bush Tomato Relish

Ingredients:

For Kangaroo Sausages:

- 1 lb (about 450g) kangaroo sausages
- 2 tablespoons olive oil
- Salt and black pepper to taste

For Bush Tomato Relish:

- 1 cup bush tomato relish
- 1 tablespoon olive oil
- 1 tablespoon balsamic vinegar
- 1 tablespoon honey
- 1 teaspoon Dijon mustard
- Salt and black pepper to taste
- Fresh parsley for garnish (optional)

Instructions:

For Kangaroo Sausages:

Preheat Grill:
- Preheat your grill to medium-high heat.

Prepare Kangaroo Sausages:
- Brush kangaroo sausages with olive oil and season with salt and black pepper.

Grill Sausages:
- Place the sausages on the preheated grill. Grill for about 12-15 minutes, turning occasionally, or until they are cooked through and have a nice char.

For Bush Tomato Relish:

Make Bush Tomato Relish:
- In a small saucepan over medium heat, combine bush tomato relish, olive oil, balsamic vinegar, honey, and Dijon mustard. Stir well.

Simmer:
- Allow the relish to simmer for about 5-7 minutes, stirring occasionally, until it thickens slightly.

Season:

- Season the bush tomato relish with salt and black pepper to taste. Adjust the sweetness or acidity if needed.

Garnish (Optional):
- Garnish with fresh parsley if desired.

Serve:
- Serve the grilled Kangaroo Sausages with a generous spoonful of Bush Tomato Relish on the side.

Enjoy:
- Enjoy this uniquely Australian dish that features kangaroo sausages paired with the rich and flavorful Bush Tomato Relish. It's a delicious combination that showcases the diverse and native flavors of Australian cuisine.

Grilled Moreton Bay Bugs with Garlic Butter

Ingredients:

For Moreton Bay Bugs:

- 4 Moreton Bay Bugs
- 2 tablespoons olive oil
- Salt and black pepper to taste
- Lemon wedges for serving

For Garlic Butter Sauce:

- 1/2 cup unsalted butter, melted
- 4 cloves garlic, minced
- 1 tablespoon fresh parsley, finely chopped
- 1 teaspoon lemon juice
- Salt and black pepper to taste

Instructions:

For Moreton Bay Bugs:

Prepare Bugs:
- Rinse the Moreton Bay Bugs under cold water. Using kitchen shears, cut along the center of the underside of each bug to expose the meat.

Season Bugs:
- Brush the bugs with olive oil and season with salt and black pepper.

Grill Bugs:
- Preheat your grill to medium-high heat. Place the bugs on the grill, shell side down, and cook for about 3-4 minutes.

Flip and Cook:
- Flip the bugs and cook for an additional 3-4 minutes or until the meat is opaque and cooked through. Be cautious not to overcook.

For Garlic Butter Sauce:

Make Garlic Butter Sauce:
- In a small saucepan or microwave-safe bowl, combine melted butter, minced garlic, chopped fresh parsley, lemon juice, salt, and black pepper. Mix well.

Brush Bugs:

- Brush the grilled Moreton Bay Bugs generously with the garlic butter sauce while they are still hot.

Serve:
- Transfer the bugs to a serving platter, drizzle any remaining garlic butter sauce over them, and serve with lemon wedges on the side.

Enjoy:
- Enjoy these Grilled Moreton Bay Bugs with Garlic Butter as a delightful seafood dish, perfect for a barbecue or special occasion. The garlic butter enhances the natural flavors of the bugs for a delicious and indulgent experience.

BBQ Lamb Chops with Mint Sauce

Ingredients:

For BBQ Lamb Chops:

- 8 lamb chops
- 2 tablespoons olive oil
- 2 cloves garlic, minced
- 1 teaspoon dried rosemary
- 1 teaspoon dried thyme
- Salt and black pepper to taste

For Mint Sauce:

- 1/2 cup fresh mint leaves, finely chopped
- 2 tablespoons red wine vinegar
- 1 tablespoon honey
- 2 tablespoons olive oil
- Salt and black pepper to taste

Instructions:

For BBQ Lamb Chops:

Prepare Lamb Chops:
- Pat the lamb chops dry with paper towels. Place them in a bowl.

Marinate Lamb Chops:
- In a small bowl, mix together olive oil, minced garlic, dried rosemary, dried thyme, salt, and black pepper. Pour this marinade over the lamb chops, ensuring each chop is well-coated. Let them marinate for at least 30 minutes to allow the flavors to infuse.

Preheat Grill:
- Preheat your grill to medium-high heat.

Grill Lamb Chops:
- Place the marinated lamb chops on the preheated grill. Grill for about 3-4 minutes per side for medium-rare, or adjust the cooking time based on your desired doneness.

Rest:
- Remove the lamb chops from the grill and let them rest for a few minutes before serving.

For Mint Sauce:

Prepare Mint Sauce:
- In a small bowl, combine finely chopped fresh mint leaves, red wine vinegar, honey, olive oil, salt, and black pepper. Mix well to create the mint sauce.

Serve:
- Arrange the grilled lamb chops on a serving platter. Drizzle the mint sauce over the chops or serve it on the side as a dipping sauce.

Garnish (Optional):
- Garnish with additional fresh mint leaves for a burst of color.

Enjoy:
- Serve these BBQ Lamb Chops with Mint Sauce for a flavorful and aromatic experience. The combination of grilled lamb and mint sauce is a classic and delightful pairing.

Vegemite-Marinated Shrimp Skewers

Ingredients:

For Vegemite Marinade:

- 2 tablespoons Vegemite
- 2 tablespoons honey
- 2 tablespoons olive oil
- 2 cloves garlic, minced
- 1 tablespoon lemon juice
- 1 teaspoon soy sauce
- 1 teaspoon smoked paprika
- Salt and black pepper to taste

For Shrimp Skewers:

- 1 lb (450g) large shrimp, peeled and deveined
- Wooden or metal skewers, soaked if wooden

Instructions:

For Vegemite Marinade:

Prepare Marinade:
- In a bowl, whisk together Vegemite, honey, olive oil, minced garlic, lemon juice, soy sauce, smoked paprika, salt, and black pepper. Ensure the Vegemite is well incorporated into the marinade.

Marinate Shrimp:
- Place the peeled and deveined shrimp in a shallow dish or a zip-top bag. Pour the Vegemite marinade over the shrimp, ensuring they are well-coated. Marinate in the refrigerator for at least 30 minutes, allowing the flavors to infuse.

For Shrimp Skewers:

Preheat Grill:
- Preheat your grill to medium-high heat.

Skewer Shrimp:
- Thread the marinated shrimp onto the skewers, ensuring an even distribution.

Grill Shrimp Skewers:
- Place the shrimp skewers on the preheated grill. Grill for about 2-3 minutes per side or until the shrimp are opaque and have a nice char.

Baste with Marinade:
- During grilling, baste the shrimp skewers with additional Vegemite marinade for added flavor.

Serve:
- Once the shrimp are cooked through, remove them from the grill and serve immediately.

Garnish (Optional):
- Garnish with a squeeze of fresh lemon juice and chopped parsley for a bright and fresh touch.

Enjoy:
- Enjoy these Vegemite-Marinated Shrimp Skewers as a unique and flavorful appetizer or main dish. The Vegemite adds a savory depth of flavor to the shrimp, creating a delicious and memorable dish.

BBQ Kangaroo Kebabs with Lemon Myrtle

Ingredients:

For Kangaroo Kebabs:

- 1 lb (450g) kangaroo meat, cut into cubes
- 1 red bell pepper, cut into chunks
- 1 yellow bell pepper, cut into chunks
- 1 red onion, cut into chunks
- Cherry tomatoes
- Wooden or metal skewers, soaked if wooden

For Marinade:

- 2 tablespoons olive oil
- 2 tablespoons lemon myrtle seasoning
- 2 cloves garlic, minced
- 1 tablespoon honey
- 1 tablespoon soy sauce
- Salt and black pepper to taste

Instructions:

Prepare Marinade:
- In a bowl, whisk together olive oil, lemon myrtle seasoning, minced garlic, honey, soy sauce, salt, and black pepper to create the marinade.

Marinate Kangaroo Meat:
- Place the kangaroo meat cubes in a shallow dish or a zip-top bag. Pour the marinade over the meat, ensuring it is well-coated. Marinate in the refrigerator for at least 1-2 hours, allowing the flavors to meld.

Assemble Kebabs:
- Preheat your grill to medium-high heat. Thread the marinated kangaroo meat, bell peppers, red onion, and cherry tomatoes onto the skewers, creating kebabs.

Grill Kebabs:
- Place the kangaroo kebabs on the preheated grill. Grill for about 4-5 minutes per side or until the kangaroo meat is cooked to your desired level of doneness and the vegetables are tender.

Baste with Marinade:

- During grilling, baste the kebabs with the remaining marinade for additional flavor.

Serve:
- Once the kangaroo kebabs are cooked through, remove them from the grill and let them rest for a few minutes.

Garnish (Optional):
- Garnish with a sprinkle of additional lemon myrtle seasoning for a burst of citrusy aroma.

Enjoy:
- Serve these BBQ Kangaroo Kebabs with Lemon Myrtle as a unique and flavorful dish. The lemon myrtle seasoning adds a distinctive Australian touch to the kangaroo meat, creating a delicious and memorable meal.

Salads and Sides:

Aussie Potato Salad

Ingredients:

- 2 lbs (about 1 kg) potatoes, peeled and diced
- 4 hard-boiled eggs, chopped
- 1 cup mayonnaise
- 2 tablespoons white vinegar
- 1 tablespoon Dijon mustard
- 1 small red onion, finely chopped
- 3 celery stalks, finely chopped
- 1/4 cup fresh parsley, chopped
- Salt and black pepper to taste
- Paprika for garnish (optional)

Instructions:

Boil Potatoes:
- In a large pot, bring salted water to a boil. Add the diced potatoes and cook until they are fork-tender. Drain and let them cool.

Prepare Dressing:
- In a small bowl, whisk together mayonnaise, white vinegar, Dijon mustard, salt, and black pepper to create the dressing.

Assemble Salad:
- In a large mixing bowl, combine the cooled diced potatoes, chopped hard-boiled eggs, finely chopped red onion, celery, and fresh parsley.

Add Dressing:
- Pour the prepared dressing over the potato mixture. Gently toss until the ingredients are evenly coated with the dressing.

Adjust Seasoning:
- Taste the potato salad and adjust the salt and pepper according to your preference.

Chill:
- Cover the bowl and refrigerate the potato salad for at least 2 hours to allow the flavors to meld and the salad to chill.

Garnish and Serve:

- Before serving, garnish the Aussie Potato Salad with a sprinkle of paprika for a pop of color.

Enjoy:

- Serve the Aussie Potato Salad as a refreshing side dish at barbecues, picnics, or any Australian-inspired gathering. It's a classic and hearty salad that complements various mains.

Grilled Asparagus with Lemon Myrtle Butter

Ingredients:

- 1 bunch fresh asparagus spears, trimmed
- 2 tablespoons unsalted butter, melted
- 1 teaspoon lemon myrtle seasoning
- Zest of one lemon
- Salt and black pepper to taste
- Lemon wedges for serving

Instructions:

Preheat Grill:
- Preheat your grill to medium-high heat.

Prepare Asparagus:
- Trim the tough ends of the asparagus spears.

Make Lemon Myrtle Butter:
- In a small bowl, mix melted unsalted butter with lemon myrtle seasoning, lemon zest, salt, and black pepper. Stir well to combine.

Grill Asparagus:
- Place the trimmed asparagus spears on the preheated grill. Grill for about 3-4 minutes, turning occasionally, until they are tender and slightly charred.

Brush with Lemon Myrtle Butter:
- During the last minute of grilling, brush the asparagus spears with the prepared lemon myrtle butter, ensuring they are well-coated.

Serve:
- Transfer the grilled asparagus to a serving platter.

Garnish (Optional):
- Garnish with additional lemon zest for a burst of freshness.

Serve with Lemon Wedges:
- Serve the Grilled Asparagus with Lemon Myrtle Butter with lemon wedges on the side for an extra squeeze of citrus flavor.

Enjoy:
- Enjoy this simple and flavorful side dish as a complement to your main course. The combination of grilled asparagus with the aromatic lemon myrtle butter creates a delicious and vibrant dish.

Rocket and Parmesan Salad with Macadamia Dressing

Ingredients:

For Salad:

- 4 cups fresh rocket (arugula) leaves, washed and dried
- 1/2 cup shaved Parmesan cheese
- 1/4 cup toasted macadamia nuts, chopped

For Macadamia Dressing:

- 1/2 cup macadamia nuts, toasted
- 1/4 cup extra-virgin olive oil
- 2 tablespoons white wine vinegar
- 1 clove garlic, minced
- Salt and black pepper to taste
- Water (as needed for desired consistency)

Instructions:

For Macadamia Dressing:

  Toast Macadamia Nuts:
  - In a dry pan over medium heat, toast the macadamia nuts until they are golden brown and fragrant. Remove from heat and let them cool.

  Prepare Dressing:
  - In a blender or food processor, combine the toasted macadamia nuts, extra-virgin olive oil, white wine vinegar, minced garlic, salt, and black pepper.

  Blend:
  - Blend the ingredients until you achieve a smooth and creamy consistency. If the dressing is too thick, you can add water a little at a time until it reaches your desired thickness.

  Adjust Seasoning:
  - Taste the dressing and adjust the salt and pepper according to your preference.

  For Salad:

   Assemble Salad:

- In a large salad bowl, toss the fresh rocket leaves with the shaved Parmesan cheese.

Add Macadamia Nuts:
- Sprinkle the toasted and chopped macadamia nuts over the salad.

Drizzle Dressing:
- Drizzle the prepared macadamia dressing over the salad. Start with a portion of the dressing and add more as needed.

Toss Gently:
- Gently toss the salad until the rocket leaves are well coated with the dressing and the ingredients are evenly distributed.

Serve:
- Serve the Rocket and Parmesan Salad with Macadamia Dressing immediately as a refreshing and nutty side dish.

Enjoy:
- Enjoy this vibrant and flavorful salad that combines the peppery notes of rocket, the richness of Parmesan, and the nutty goodness of macadamia nuts, all brought together with a luscious macadamia dressing.

Coleslaw with Australian Granny Smith Apples

Ingredients:

For Coleslaw:

- 4 cups shredded green cabbage
- 1 cup shredded purple cabbage
- 2 large carrots, grated
- 2 Australian Granny Smith apples, thinly sliced
- 1/2 cup chopped fresh parsley

For Dressing:

- 1/2 cup mayonnaise
- 2 tablespoons Greek yogurt
- 2 tablespoons apple cider vinegar
- 1 tablespoon honey
- Salt and black pepper to taste

Instructions:

For Coleslaw:

Prepare Vegetables:
- Shred the green and purple cabbage, grate the carrots, thinly slice the Australian Granny Smith apples, and chop the fresh parsley.

For Dressing:

Make Dressing:
- In a small bowl, whisk together mayonnaise, Greek yogurt, apple cider vinegar, honey, salt, and black pepper. Mix until the dressing is smooth and well combined.

Adjust Seasoning:
- Taste the dressing and adjust the salt and pepper according to your preference. If you prefer a sweeter dressing, you can add more honey.

Assemble Coleslaw:

Combine Ingredients:

- In a large mixing bowl, combine the shredded green and purple cabbage, grated carrots, sliced Australian Granny Smith apples, and chopped fresh parsley.

Add Dressing:
- Pour the prepared dressing over the coleslaw ingredients.

Toss Gently:
- Gently toss the coleslaw until the vegetables and apples are evenly coated with the dressing.

Chill:
- Cover the bowl and refrigerate the coleslaw for at least 1-2 hours before serving. This allows the flavors to meld, and the coleslaw becomes crisp and refreshing.

Serve:
- Serve the Coleslaw with Australian Granny Smith Apples as a delightful side dish at barbecues, picnics, or any meal where you want a crunchy and tangy coleslaw with a hint of sweetness from the apples.

Enjoy:
- Enjoy this refreshing and colorful coleslaw that brings together the crispness of cabbage, the sweetness of Australian Granny Smith apples, and the creamy tanginess of the dressing.

Bush Tomato and Quinoa Salad

Ingredients:

- 1 cup quinoa, rinsed and cooked according to package instructions
- 2 tablespoons bush tomato chutney (or rehydrated bush tomatoes, chopped)
- 1 cup cherry tomatoes, halved
- 1 cucumber, diced
- 1/2 red onion, finely chopped
- 1/4 cup fresh parsley, chopped
- 1/4 cup olive oil
- 2 tablespoons red wine vinegar
- Salt and black pepper to taste
- Feta cheese, crumbled (optional, for garnish)

Instructions:

Cook Quinoa:
- Rinse the quinoa under cold water and cook it according to the package instructions. Once cooked, fluff it with a fork and let it cool.

Prepare Bush Tomato Chutney:
- If using dried bush tomatoes, rehydrate them in warm water for about 15-20 minutes, then chop them finely. Alternatively, use ready-made bush tomato chutney.

Make Dressing:
- In a small bowl, whisk together olive oil, red wine vinegar, salt, and black pepper to create the dressing.

Combine Ingredients:
- In a large mixing bowl, combine the cooked quinoa, bush tomato chutney (or chopped rehydrated bush tomatoes), halved cherry tomatoes, diced cucumber, finely chopped red onion, and chopped fresh parsley.

Add Dressing:
- Pour the prepared dressing over the quinoa mixture.

Toss Gently:
- Gently toss the salad until all ingredients are well coated with the dressing.

Chill:
- Cover the bowl and refrigerate the Bush Tomato and Quinoa Salad for at least 1-2 hours to allow the flavors to meld.

Serve:
- Before serving, garnish with crumbled feta cheese if desired.

Enjoy:
- Serve this Bush Tomato and Quinoa Salad as a nutritious and flavorful side dish. The combination of quinoa, bush tomatoes, and fresh vegetables creates a unique and delicious salad with an Australian twist.

Roasted Pumpkin and Chickpea Salad

Ingredients:

For Salad:

- 1 small pumpkin, peeled, seeded, and diced
- 1 can (15 oz) chickpeas, drained and rinsed
- 2 tablespoons olive oil
- 1 teaspoon ground cumin
- 1 teaspoon smoked paprika
- Salt and black pepper to taste
- 4 cups mixed salad greens (e.g., spinach, arugula, and watercress)
- 1/2 cup feta cheese, crumbled
- 1/4 cup pumpkin seeds, toasted
- 1/4 cup balsamic glaze (or balsamic vinegar)

Instructions:

Preheat Oven:
- Preheat the oven to 400°F (200°C).

Roast Pumpkin and Chickpeas:
- In a large bowl, toss the diced pumpkin and chickpeas with olive oil, ground cumin, smoked paprika, salt, and black pepper until well coated. Spread the mixture on a baking sheet in a single layer. Roast in the preheated oven for 25-30 minutes or until the pumpkin is tender and chickpeas are golden brown. Stir halfway through the roasting time for even cooking.

Prepare Salad Greens:
- In a large salad bowl, place the mixed salad greens.

Assemble Salad:
- Once the pumpkin and chickpeas are roasted, let them cool slightly. Add the roasted pumpkin and chickpeas to the salad greens.

Add Feta and Pumpkin Seeds:
- Sprinkle crumbled feta cheese and toasted pumpkin seeds over the salad.

Drizzle Balsamic Glaze:
- Drizzle balsamic glaze (or balsamic vinegar) over the salad.

Toss Gently:
- Gently toss the salad until all ingredients are well combined.

Serve:

- Serve the Roasted Pumpkin and Chickpea Salad as a wholesome and flavorful side dish or a light main course.

Enjoy:

- Enjoy this delicious salad that combines the sweetness of roasted pumpkin, the nuttiness of chickpeas, and the tanginess of feta cheese, all brought together with the rich flavor of balsamic glaze.

Tomato and Burrata Salad with Australian Olive Oil

Ingredients:

For Salad:

- 1 cup quinoa, rinsed and cooked according to package instructions
- 1/2 cup bush tomatoes, rehydrated if dried or halved if fresh
- 1 cucumber, diced
- 1 red bell pepper, diced
- 1/4 cup red onion, finely chopped
- 1/4 cup fresh parsley, chopped
- Salt and black pepper to taste

For Dressing:

- 3 tablespoons Australian olive oil
- 1 tablespoon lemon juice
- 1 teaspoon honey
- 1 teaspoon ground bush tomato (optional for extra flavor)
- Salt and black pepper to taste

Instructions:

Prepare Quinoa:
- Rinse quinoa under cold water and cook it according to package instructions. Once cooked, let it cool to room temperature.

Rehydrate Bush Tomatoes:
- If using dried bush tomatoes, rehydrate them in warm water according to the package instructions. If using fresh bush tomatoes, simply halve them.

Prepare Vegetables:
- In a large bowl, combine the cooked quinoa, rehydrated or fresh bush tomatoes, diced cucumber, diced red bell pepper, finely chopped red onion, and chopped fresh parsley.

Make Dressing:
- In a small bowl, whisk together Australian olive oil, lemon juice, honey, ground bush tomato (if using), salt, and black pepper. Mix well to create the dressing.

Combine Salad and Dressing:
- Pour the dressing over the quinoa and vegetable mixture. Gently toss until all ingredients are well coated with the dressing.

Adjust Seasoning:
- Taste the salad and adjust the salt and pepper according to your preference.

Chill (Optional):
- For enhanced flavors, cover the salad and refrigerate for at least 30 minutes before serving.

Serve:
- Serve the Bush Tomato and Quinoa Salad as a nutritious and flavorful side dish or a light main course.

Enjoy:
- Enjoy the unique blend of bush tomatoes and quinoa, complemented by the freshness of vegetables and the savory Australian olive oil dressing.

Dips and Spreads:

Macadamia and Bush Tomato Pesto

Ingredients:

- 1 cup roasted and unsalted macadamia nuts
- 1/2 cup sun-dried bush tomatoes (rehydrated in warm water if dried)
- 2 cloves garlic, peeled
- 1 cup fresh basil leaves
- 1/2 cup freshly grated Parmesan cheese
- 1/2 cup Australian extra-virgin olive oil
- Salt and black pepper to taste
- Lemon juice (optional, for extra brightness)

Instructions:

Prepare Macadamia Nuts:
- If the macadamia nuts are not already roasted, roast them in a dry pan over medium heat until they are golden brown and fragrant. Let them cool.

Rehydrate Bush Tomatoes:
- If using dried bush tomatoes, rehydrate them in warm water according to the package instructions. If using sun-dried tomatoes in oil, drain any excess oil.

Combine Ingredients:
- In a food processor, combine the roasted macadamia nuts, rehydrated bush tomatoes, peeled garlic cloves, fresh basil leaves, and freshly grated Parmesan cheese.

Pulse:
- Pulse the ingredients until they are coarsely chopped.

Add Olive Oil:
- With the food processor running, gradually pour in the Australian extra-virgin olive oil in a steady stream. Continue processing until the mixture reaches your desired consistency.

Season:
- Season the pesto with salt and black pepper. If you like, add a squeeze of lemon juice for extra brightness.

Adjust Consistency (Optional):

- If the pesto is too thick, you can add more olive oil until you achieve the desired thickness.

Taste and Adjust:
- Taste the pesto and adjust the seasoning, adding more salt, pepper, or lemon juice as needed.

Store or Serve:
- Transfer the Macadamia and Bush Tomato Pesto to a jar and store it in the refrigerator for up to a week. Alternatively, use it immediately.

Enjoy:
- Enjoy this unique and flavorful Macadamia and Bush Tomato Pesto on pasta, as a spread, or as a dip. The combination of macadamia nuts and bush tomatoes creates a rich and nutty pesto with an Australian twist.

Beetroot and Horseradish Dip

Ingredients:

- 2 medium-sized beetroots, roasted and peeled
- 1/2 cup Greek yogurt
- 2 tablespoons horseradish (adjust to taste)
- 1 clove garlic, minced
- 1 tablespoon lemon juice
- Salt and black pepper to taste
- Fresh dill for garnish (optional)

Instructions:

Roast and Peel Beetroots:
- Preheat the oven to 400°F (200°C). Wrap the beetroots in foil and roast in the oven until they are tender (usually about 45-60 minutes). Once cooked, let them cool, peel, and dice.

Prepare Beetroots:
- In a food processor, add the roasted and peeled beetroots. Pulse until they are finely chopped.

Combine Ingredients:
- Add Greek yogurt, horseradish, minced garlic, and lemon juice to the processed beetroots.

Blend:
- Blend the ingredients until you achieve a smooth and well-combined consistency.

Season:
- Season the dip with salt and black pepper. Adjust the horseradish quantity to your taste preferences.

Garnish (Optional):
- Garnish the dip with fresh dill for added flavor and a pop of color.

Chill (Optional):
- For enhanced flavors, refrigerate the dip for at least 30 minutes before serving.

Serve:
- Serve the Beetroot and Horseradish Dip with your favorite crackers, vegetable sticks, or as a spread for bread.

Enjoy:

- Enjoy this vibrant and flavorful dip that combines the earthy sweetness of beetroots with the zesty kick of horseradish. It's a perfect appetizer or snack for any occasion.

Avocado and Vegemite Dip

Ingredients:

- 2 ripe avocados, peeled and pitted
- 2 teaspoons Vegemite (adjust to taste)
- 1 tablespoon lemon juice
- 1 clove garlic, minced
- 2 tablespoons Greek yogurt
- Salt and black pepper to taste
- Toasted whole-grain bread or vegetable sticks (for serving)

Instructions:

Prepare Avocados:
- In a bowl, mash the ripe avocados with a fork until you achieve a smooth consistency.

Add Vegemite:
- Add Vegemite to the mashed avocados. Start with a small amount and adjust to your taste preferences. Vegemite is strong, so a little goes a long way.

Incorporate Other Ingredients:
- Add lemon juice, minced garlic, and Greek yogurt to the avocado mixture. Mix well to combine all the ingredients.

Season:
- Season the dip with salt and black pepper according to your taste.

Adjust Consistency (Optional):
- If the dip is too thick, you can add a bit more Greek yogurt or lemon juice to achieve your desired consistency.

Taste and Adjust:
- Taste the Avocado and Vegemite Dip and adjust the Vegemite or other seasonings if needed.

Serve:
- Transfer the dip to a serving bowl.

Garnish (Optional):
- Garnish with a drizzle of olive oil, a sprinkle of black sesame seeds, or chopped fresh herbs for added flavor and presentation.

Serve with Toast or Vegetables:
- Serve the Avocado and Vegemite Dip with toasted whole-grain bread or vegetable sticks.

Enjoy:
- Enjoy this unique and savory dip that combines the creamy goodness of avocado with the umami richness of Vegemite. It's a delightful spread for a quick snack or appetizer.

Lemon Myrtle Hummus

Ingredients:

- 1 can (15 oz) chickpeas, drained and rinsed
- 1/4 cup tahini
- 1/4 cup fresh lemon juice
- 2 tablespoons Australian extra-virgin olive oil
- 1 clove garlic, minced
- 1 teaspoon ground cumin
- 1 teaspoon lemon myrtle seasoning
- Salt and black pepper to taste
- Water (as needed for desired consistency)
- Lemon wedges and olive oil for garnish (optional)

Instructions:

Prepare Chickpeas:
- Drain and rinse the canned chickpeas thoroughly.

Combine Ingredients:
- In a food processor, combine chickpeas, tahini, fresh lemon juice, Australian extra-virgin olive oil, minced garlic, ground cumin, and lemon myrtle seasoning.

Blend:
- Blend the ingredients until you get a smooth and creamy consistency. If the mixture is too thick, you can add water, a tablespoon at a time, until you achieve your desired consistency.

Season:
- Season the hummus with salt and black pepper to taste. Adjust the lemon myrtle seasoning if needed.

Adjust Consistency (Optional):
- If the hummus is too thick, add more water or olive oil and blend until smooth.

Taste and Adjust:
- Taste the Lemon Myrtle Hummus and adjust the seasoning, lemon juice, or other ingredients to suit your preference.

Serve:
- Transfer the hummus to a serving bowl.

Garnish (Optional):

- Garnish with a drizzle of olive oil, a sprinkle of lemon myrtle seasoning, and a few lemon wedges for an extra burst of citrus flavor.

Serve with Pita or Vegetables:

- Serve the Lemon Myrtle Hummus with pita bread, vegetable sticks, or your favorite crackers.

Enjoy:

- Enjoy this flavorful and aromatic hummus with a unique Australian twist. The lemon myrtle seasoning adds a citrusy note that complements the creamy texture of the hummus.

Australian Bush Salsa with Native Herbs

Ingredients:

- 2 tomatoes, diced
- 1 red onion, finely chopped
- 2 tablespoons lemon myrtle leaves, finely chopped
- 1 tablespoon riberry (lilly pilly), chopped
- 1 tablespoon wattleseed, roasted
- 1 tablespoon bush tomatoes, rehydrated if dried and chopped
- 1 tablespoon olive oil
- 1 tablespoon balsamic vinegar
- Salt and pepper to taste

Instructions:

Prepare Ingredients:
- Dice the tomatoes, finely chop the red onion, lemon myrtle leaves, riberry, and bush tomatoes.

Roast Wattleseed:
- If not already roasted, lightly roast the wattleseed in a dry pan over medium heat until it becomes fragrant. Let it cool.

Rehydrate Bush Tomatoes (if needed):
- If using dried bush tomatoes, rehydrate them in warm water according to the package instructions.

Combine Ingredients:
- In a bowl, combine the diced tomatoes, finely chopped red onion, lemon myrtle leaves, riberry, and chopped bush tomatoes.

Add Wattleseed:
- Add the roasted wattleseed to the salsa mixture.

Dress the Salsa:
- Drizzle olive oil and balsamic vinegar over the ingredients.

Season:
- Season the salsa with salt and pepper according to your taste preferences.

Mix Well:
- Gently toss all the ingredients until well combined.

Chill (Optional):
- For enhanced flavors, cover the bowl and refrigerate the salsa for at least 30 minutes before serving.

Serve:
- Serve the Australian Bush Salsa with Native Herbs as a refreshing condiment or topping for grilled meats, seafood, or as a dip with tortilla chips.

Enjoy:
- Enjoy the unique flavors of native Australian herbs in this vibrant salsa, providing a taste of the Australian bush in every bite.

Pasta and Noodles:

Pumpkin Gnocchi with Sage Butter

Ingredients:

For Pumpkin Gnocchi:

- 2 cups pumpkin puree (cooked and mashed)
- 2 cups potato, cooked and mashed
- 2 1/2 - 3 cups all-purpose flour
- 1/2 cup grated Parmesan cheese
- 1 teaspoon salt
- 1/2 teaspoon ground nutmeg

For Sage Butter Sauce:

- 1/2 cup unsalted butter
- Fresh sage leaves
- Salt and black pepper to taste
- Grated Parmesan cheese (for garnish)

Instructions:

For Pumpkin Gnocchi:

Prepare Pumpkin and Potatoes:
- Cook the pumpkin and potatoes until they are tender. Mash them thoroughly and let them cool.

Make Gnocchi Dough:
- In a large bowl, combine the mashed pumpkin and potatoes. Add grated Parmesan cheese, salt, and ground nutmeg. Gradually add the flour, kneading the dough until it comes together and is no longer sticky.

Form Gnocchi:
- Divide the dough into smaller portions. Roll each portion into a long rope and cut it into bite-sized pieces. Optionally, use a fork to create ridges on the gnocchi.

Boil Gnocchi:

- Bring a large pot of salted water to a boil. Cook the gnocchi in batches until they float to the surface. Remove them with a slotted spoon and set aside.

For Sage Butter Sauce:

Sage Butter:
- In a skillet, melt unsalted butter over medium heat. Add fresh sage leaves and let them cook until the butter starts to brown slightly, and the sage becomes crispy.

Toss Gnocchi:
- Add the cooked pumpkin gnocchi to the sage butter sauce. Toss gently until the gnocchi are coated with the sage-infused butter.

Season:
- Season with salt and black pepper to taste.

Serve:
- Transfer the Pumpkin Gnocchi with Sage Butter to a serving dish. Garnish with additional Parmesan cheese.

Enjoy:
- Enjoy this delicious and comforting dish, featuring light and pillowy pumpkin gnocchi coated in a flavorful sage-infused butter sauce.

Crab Linguine with Finger Lime

Ingredients:

- 8 oz linguine pasta
- 1 tablespoon olive oil
- 2 cloves garlic, minced
- 1 red chili, finely chopped (adjust to taste)
- 1 pound fresh crab meat, picked and cleaned
- Zest of 1 lemon
- Juice of 1 lemon
- 2 tablespoons fresh parsley, chopped
- Salt and black pepper to taste
- Finger limes for garnish

Instructions:

Cook Linguine:
- Cook the linguine pasta in a large pot of salted boiling water according to the package instructions. Drain and set aside.

Prepare Crab Mixture:
- In a large skillet, heat olive oil over medium heat. Add minced garlic and chopped red chili. Sauté for a minute until fragrant.

Add Crab Meat:
- Add the fresh crab meat to the skillet. Cook for 2-3 minutes, stirring gently, until the crab is heated through.

Season:
- Season the crab mixture with salt, black pepper, and lemon zest. Stir to combine.

Add Linguine:
- Add the cooked linguine to the skillet with the crab mixture.

Lemon Juice:
- Squeeze the juice of one lemon over the linguine and crab. Toss the ingredients to coat the pasta evenly.

Fresh Parsley:
- Sprinkle chopped fresh parsley over the linguine and crab mixture. Toss again to incorporate.

Serve:
- Transfer the Crab Linguine with Finger Lime to serving plates.

Garnish:

- Cut the finger limes in half and gently squeeze the pearls over the linguine as a garnish. The finger limes add a burst of citrus flavor and unique texture.

Enjoy:

- Serve immediately and enjoy this delightful and fresh Crab Linguine with the unique addition of finger limes for a burst of citrusy goodness.

Spaghetti Carbonara with Australian Bacon

Ingredients:

- 12 oz (340g) spaghetti
- 1 tablespoon olive oil
- 8 oz (225g) Australian bacon, diced
- 3 large eggs
- 1 cup freshly grated Parmesan cheese
- 2 cloves garlic, minced
- Salt and black pepper to taste
- Fresh parsley, chopped (for garnish)

Instructions:

Cook Spaghetti:
- Cook the spaghetti in a large pot of salted boiling water according to the package instructions. Reserve a cup of pasta cooking water before draining.

Cook Australian Bacon:
- In a large skillet, heat olive oil over medium heat. Add the diced Australian bacon and cook until it becomes crispy and golden brown. Remove excess fat if necessary.

Prepare Carbonara Sauce:
- In a bowl, whisk together the eggs, grated Parmesan cheese, minced garlic, salt, and black pepper.

Combine Ingredients:
- Once the spaghetti is cooked, drain it and immediately add it to the skillet with the cooked bacon. Toss to combine.

Add Carbonara Sauce:
- Quickly pour the carbonara sauce over the hot spaghetti and toss thoroughly. The heat from the pasta will cook the eggs and create a creamy sauce. If needed, add a bit of the reserved pasta cooking water to achieve the desired consistency.

Season:
- Taste and adjust the seasoning with salt and black pepper.

Garnish:
- Garnish the Spaghetti Carbonara with chopped fresh parsley for a burst of freshness.

Serve:

- Plate the Spaghetti Carbonara with Australian Bacon, ensuring each serving has a generous amount of bacon and a sprinkle of Parmesan.

Enjoy:
- Serve immediately and enjoy the rich and creamy goodness of this classic pasta dish with the unique flavor of Australian bacon.

Desserts:

Pavlova with Fresh Berries

Ingredients:

For Pavlova:

- 4 large egg whites, at room temperature
- 1 cup granulated sugar
- 1 teaspoon white vinegar
- 1 teaspoon cornstarch
- 1 teaspoon vanilla extract

For Topping:

- 1 cup whipped cream
- Fresh berries (strawberries, blueberries, raspberries)
- Mint leaves for garnish
- Passion fruit pulp (optional)

Instructions:

For Pavlova:

Preheat Oven:
- Preheat your oven to 300°F (150°C). Line a baking sheet with parchment paper.

Prepare Egg Whites:
- In a clean, dry bowl, beat the egg whites with an electric mixer until stiff peaks form.

Add Sugar:
- Gradually add the granulated sugar, one tablespoon at a time, while continuing to beat the egg whites. Continue until the mixture is glossy and the sugar is fully dissolved.

Incorporate Vinegar and Cornstarch:
- Gently fold in the white vinegar, cornstarch, and vanilla extract into the meringue mixture.

Shape Pavlova:

- Spoon the meringue onto the prepared baking sheet, shaping it into a round pavlova nest. You can create a slight well in the center to hold the toppings.

Bake:
- Place the baking sheet in the preheated oven and immediately reduce the temperature to 250°F (120°C). Bake for 1.5 to 2 hours or until the pavlova is crisp on the outside and soft on the inside. Let it cool completely.

Assembling Pavlova:

Whip Cream:
- Whip the cream until stiff peaks form.

Top Pavlova:
- Spoon the whipped cream onto the center of the pavlova. Top with fresh berries of your choice, arranging them on the cream.

Garnish:
- Garnish with mint leaves and, if desired, drizzle passion fruit pulp over the top.

Serve:
- Carefully transfer the Pavlova with Fresh Berries to a serving plate.

Enjoy:
- Serve slices of this delightful pavlova and enjoy the combination of crispy meringue, fluffy whipped cream, and the burst of freshness from the berries.

Lamington Ice Cream Sandwiches

Ingredients:

For Lamingtons:

- 2 cups all-purpose flour
- 2 teaspoons baking powder
- 1/2 teaspoon salt
- 1/2 cup unsalted butter, softened
- 1 cup granulated sugar
- 3 large eggs
- 1 teaspoon vanilla extract
- 1 cup milk

For Ice Cream Filling:

- Vanilla ice cream
- Shredded coconut (for coating)

Instructions:

For Lamingtons:

Preheat Oven:
- Preheat your oven to 350°F (180°C). Grease and flour a square baking pan.

Mix Dry Ingredients:
- In a bowl, whisk together the all-purpose flour, baking powder, and salt. Set aside.

Cream Butter and Sugar:
- In a large bowl, cream together the softened butter and granulated sugar until light and fluffy.

Add Eggs and Vanilla:
- Add the eggs one at a time, beating well after each addition. Stir in the vanilla extract.

Alternate Flour and Milk:
- Gradually add the dry ingredients to the wet ingredients, alternating with the milk. Begin and end with the dry ingredients, mixing until just combined.

Bake:
- Pour the batter into the prepared baking pan and smooth the top. Bake in the preheated oven for 25-30 minutes or until a toothpick inserted into the center comes out clean. Let it cool completely.

Cut into Squares:

- Once cooled, cut the cake into squares of your desired size.

Assembling Lamington Ice Cream Sandwiches:

Prepare Ice Cream Filling:
- Soften the vanilla ice cream to a spreadable consistency.

Assemble Ice Cream Sandwiches:
- Take one square of the Lamington and spread a layer of softened vanilla ice cream on top. Place another Lamington square on top to create a sandwich.

Coat with Shredded Coconut:
- Roll the edges of the ice cream sandwich in shredded coconut until well-coated.

Freeze:
- Place the assembled Lamington Ice Cream Sandwiches in the freezer for at least 2 hours or until the ice cream is firm.

Serve:
- Serve the Lamington Ice Cream Sandwiches chilled and enjoy this delightful Australian twist on a classic treat.

Enjoy:
- Indulge in the sweet and coconut-covered goodness of Lamington Ice Cream Sandwiches.

Wattleseed Chocolate Brownies

Ingredients:

- 1 cup unsalted butter, melted
- 2 cups granulated sugar
- 4 large eggs
- 1 teaspoon vanilla extract
- 1 cup all-purpose flour
- 1/2 cup wattleseed powder
- 1/2 cup cocoa powder
- 1/2 teaspoon baking powder
- 1/4 teaspoon salt
- 1 cup chocolate chips or chunks
- Chopped nuts (optional)

Instructions:

Preheat Oven:
- Preheat your oven to 350°F (175°C). Grease and line a baking pan with parchment paper.

Melt Butter:
- In a microwave-safe bowl, melt the unsalted butter.

Mix Sugar and Eggs:
- In a large mixing bowl, whisk together the granulated sugar and eggs until well combined.

Add Melted Butter and Vanilla:
- Pour the melted butter into the sugar and egg mixture. Add vanilla extract and mix until smooth.

Combine Dry Ingredients:
- In a separate bowl, sift together the all-purpose flour, wattleseed powder, cocoa powder, baking powder, and salt.

Incorporate Dry Ingredients:
- Gradually add the dry ingredients to the wet ingredients, stirring until just combined. Be careful not to overmix.

Add Chocolate Chips and Nuts:
- Fold in the chocolate chips or chunks, and chopped nuts if using.

Transfer to Baking Pan:
- Pour the brownie batter into the prepared baking pan, spreading it evenly.

Bake:

- Bake in the preheated oven for approximately 25-30 minutes or until a toothpick inserted into the center comes out with a few moist crumbs (not wet batter).

Cool and Cut:
- Allow the brownies to cool completely in the pan before lifting them out using the parchment paper. Once cooled, cut into squares.

Serve:
- Serve these delicious Wattleseed Chocolate Brownies as a delightful treat or dessert.

Enjoy:
- Enjoy the rich, chocolatey flavor with a unique twist from the wattleseed powder!

Anzac Biscuits

Ingredients:

- 1 cup rolled oats
- 1 cup all-purpose flour
- 1 cup desiccated coconut
- 1 cup brown sugar, packed
- 1/2 cup unsalted butter
- 2 tablespoons golden syrup (or substitute with maple syrup)
- 1/2 teaspoon baking soda
- 2 tablespoons boiling water

Instructions:

Preheat Oven:
- Preheat your oven to 350°F (180°C). Line baking sheets with parchment paper.

Mix Dry Ingredients:
- In a large bowl, combine rolled oats, all-purpose flour, desiccated coconut, and brown sugar.

Melt Butter and Golden Syrup:
- In a saucepan over low heat, melt the unsalted butter and golden syrup together.

Combine Baking Soda and Water:
- In a small bowl, dissolve the baking soda in boiling water.

Combine Wet Ingredients:
- Add the baking soda mixture to the melted butter and golden syrup. Stir well.

Add Wet Ingredients to Dry Ingredients:
- Pour the wet ingredients into the bowl of dry ingredients. Mix until well combined.

Form Cookies:
- Drop spoonfuls of the mixture onto the prepared baking sheets, leaving space between each for spreading.

Bake:
- Bake in the preheated oven for 12-15 minutes or until the Anzac biscuits are golden brown.

Cool:

- Allow the biscuits to cool on the baking sheets for a few minutes before transferring them to wire racks to cool completely.

Serve:
- Serve these classic Anzac Biscuits with a cup of tea or coffee.

Store:
- Store in an airtight container once cooled to maintain freshness.

Enjoy:
- Enjoy these delicious and iconic Anzac Biscuits, a traditional Australian treat with historical significance.

Macadamia Nut Brittle

Ingredients:

- 1 cup granulated sugar
- 1/2 cup water
- 1/2 cup light corn syrup
- 1 cup roasted macadamia nuts, roughly chopped
- 2 tablespoons unsalted butter
- 1/2 teaspoon baking soda
- 1/2 teaspoon vanilla extract
- Pinch of salt

Instructions:

Prepare Baking Sheet:
- Line a baking sheet with parchment paper and set aside.

Roast Macadamia Nuts:
- If your macadamia nuts are not already roasted, spread them on a baking sheet and roast in a preheated oven at 350°F (180°C) for about 8-10 minutes or until they are golden and fragrant. Let them cool before chopping.

Combine Sugar, Water, and Corn Syrup:
- In a medium saucepan, combine granulated sugar, water, and light corn syrup. Stir over medium heat until the sugar dissolves.

Cook to Hard Crack Stage:
- Bring the mixture to a boil and cook, without stirring, until it reaches the hard crack stage, which is around 300°F (150°C) on a candy thermometer.

Add Macadamia Nuts:
- Once at the hard crack stage, stir in the chopped roasted macadamia nuts. Be cautious, as the mixture will bubble up.

Add Butter, Baking Soda, Vanilla, and Salt:
- Add the unsalted butter, baking soda, vanilla extract, and a pinch of salt. Stir quickly to combine. The mixture will foam up.

Pour onto Baking Sheet:
- Immediately pour the hot mixture onto the prepared baking sheet, spreading it out with a spatula to your desired thickness.

Cool and Break into Pieces:
- Let the macadamia nut brittle cool completely. Once cooled and hardened, break it into pieces.

Store:
- Store the macadamia nut brittle in an airtight container at room temperature.

Enjoy:
- Enjoy this crunchy and sweet Macadamia Nut Brittle as a delightful treat or a homemade gift.

Tim Tam Cheesecake

Ingredients:

For the Crust:

- 2 cups Tim Tam crumbs (about 16-20 biscuits)
- 1/2 cup unsalted butter, melted

For the Cheesecake Filling:

- 24 oz (680g) cream cheese, softened
- 1 cup granulated sugar
- 1 teaspoon vanilla extract
- 4 large eggs
- 1 cup sour cream
- 1 cup crushed Tim Tams (for added texture)

For the Chocolate Ganache:

- 1 cup heavy cream
- 8 oz (225g) dark chocolate, finely chopped
- 2 tablespoons unsalted butter

For Garnish (Optional):

- Additional Tim Tams, crushed or whole
- Whipped cream

Instructions:

For the Crust:

    Preheat Oven:
- Preheat your oven to 325°F (160°C). Grease the bottom of a springform pan.

    Crush Tim Tams:
- In a food processor, pulse the Tim Tams until you get fine crumbs.

    Combine with Melted Butter:
- Mix the Tim Tam crumbs with melted unsalted butter until well combined.

    Press into Pan:
- Press the mixture into the bottom of the prepared springform pan to create an even crust.

    Bake:

- Bake the crust in the preheated oven for about 10 minutes. Remove and let it cool while you prepare the cheesecake filling.

For the Cheesecake Filling:

Prepare Cream Cheese Mixture:
- In a large bowl, beat the softened cream cheese until smooth. Add sugar and vanilla extract, continuing to beat until well combined.

Add Eggs:
- Add the eggs one at a time, mixing well after each addition.

Incorporate Sour Cream:
- Fold in the sour cream until the mixture is smooth.

Fold in Crushed Tim Tams:
- Gently fold in the crushed Tim Tams to distribute them evenly in the cheesecake batter.

Pour into Crust:
- Pour the cream cheese mixture over the prepared Tim Tam crust in the springform pan.

Bake:
- Bake in the preheated oven for about 50-60 minutes or until the center is set. The edges should be slightly golden.

Cool and Chill:
- Allow the cheesecake to cool in the pan, then refrigerate for several hours or overnight.

For the Chocolate Ganache:

Heat Heavy Cream:
- In a saucepan, heat the heavy cream until it just begins to simmer.

Pour over Chocolate:
- Pour the hot cream over the finely chopped dark chocolate. Let it sit for a minute, then stir until smooth.

Add Butter:
- Add butter to the chocolate ganache and stir until melted and well combined.

Cool Ganache:
- Allow the ganache to cool slightly.

Pour over Cheesecake:
- Pour the chocolate ganache over the chilled cheesecake, spreading it evenly.

Chill:
- Place the cheesecake back in the refrigerator to allow the ganache to set.

For Garnish (Optional):

Add Crushed Tim Tams and Whipped Cream:
- Before serving, garnish the Tim Tam Cheesecake with additional crushed Tim Tams and a dollop of whipped cream if desired.

Slice and Serve:
- Slice and serve this indulgent Tim Tam Cheesecake to enjoy the delicious combination of creamy cheesecake, chocolatey Tim Tams, and rich ganache.

Lemon Myrtle and Honey Panna Cotta

Ingredients:

- 2 cups heavy cream
- 1 cup whole milk
- 1/2 cup honey
- 2 tablespoons dried lemon myrtle leaves (or 4-5 fresh lemon myrtle leaves, if available)
- 1/2 cup granulated sugar
- 2 teaspoons gelatin powder
- 2 tablespoons cold water
- Fresh berries and mint leaves for garnish (optional)

Instructions:

Prepare Lemon Myrtle Infusion:
- In a saucepan, combine the heavy cream, whole milk, honey, and dried lemon myrtle leaves. If using fresh leaves, bruise them slightly before adding. Heat the mixture over medium heat until it almost reaches a simmer. Remove from heat and let it steep for 15-20 minutes to infuse the lemon myrtle flavor.

Strain Mixture:
- After steeping, strain the mixture to remove the lemon myrtle leaves. If using fresh leaves, ensure you remove them completely.

Combine Sugar:
- In a clean saucepan, combine the infused cream mixture with granulated sugar. Heat it over medium heat, stirring until the sugar dissolves. Bring the mixture to a gentle simmer.

Dissolve Gelatin:
- In a small bowl, sprinkle the gelatin powder over cold water and let it sit for a couple of minutes to bloom. Then, heat the bowl briefly in the microwave or over a pot of hot water until the gelatin is fully dissolved.

Incorporate Gelatin:
- Add the dissolved gelatin to the cream mixture, stirring well to combine. Continue heating until the mixture is thoroughly heated, but do not boil.

Cool Slightly:
- Allow the mixture to cool for a few minutes.

Pour into Molds:

- Pour the slightly cooled lemon myrtle and honey cream mixture into individual ramekins or molds.

Chill:
- Place the ramekins in the refrigerator and let the panna cotta set for at least 4 hours or overnight.

Garnish (Optional):
- Before serving, garnish the Lemon Myrtle and Honey Panna Cotta with fresh berries and mint leaves if desired.

Serve:
- Serve chilled, and enjoy the delicate citrus and honey flavors of this unique panna cotta.

Note:
- If using fresh lemon myrtle leaves, you can leave a few for garnish after straining for a decorative touch.

Drinks:

Australian Iced Coffee

Ingredients:

- 1 cup strong brewed coffee, cooled
- 1 cup milk
- 1-2 tablespoons sweetened condensed milk (adjust to taste)
- Ice cubes
- Whipped cream (optional, for garnish)
- Cocoa powder or chocolate shavings (optional, for garnish)

Instructions:

Brew Strong Coffee:
- Brew a cup of strong coffee. You can use your preferred method, such as drip, French press, or espresso.

Cool Coffee:
- Allow the brewed coffee to cool to room temperature, then refrigerate until cold. You can also use leftover coffee that has been chilled.

Prepare Milk Mixture:
- In a separate container, mix together the milk and sweetened condensed milk. Adjust the amount of sweetened condensed milk to achieve your desired level of sweetness.

Assemble Iced Coffee:
- Fill a glass with ice cubes.

Pour Coffee:
- Pour the cooled brewed coffee over the ice.

Add Milk Mixture:
- Slowly pour the milk and sweetened condensed milk mixture over the coffee. Stir gently with a long spoon to combine.

Garnish (Optional):
- If desired, top the Australian Iced Coffee with a dollop of whipped cream and sprinkle with cocoa powder or chocolate shavings.

Serve Immediately:
- Serve the Australian Iced Coffee immediately while it's cold and refreshing.

Enjoy:

- Enjoy this delicious and creamy iced coffee with a unique twist from the sweetened condensed milk.

Eucalyptus and Mint Lemonade

Ingredients:

- 1 cup fresh lemon juice (about 4-6 lemons)
- 1/2 cup honey or simple syrup (adjust to taste)
- 6-8 fresh mint leaves
- 1-2 drops of food-grade eucalyptus oil or 1 tablespoon eucalyptus syrup (adjust to taste)
- 4 cups cold water
- Ice cubes
- Lemon slices and mint sprigs for garnish

Instructions:

Prepare Fresh Lemon Juice:
- Squeeze enough lemons to yield 1 cup of fresh lemon juice.

Make Simple Syrup (If not using honey):
- If using simple syrup, combine equal parts water and sugar in a saucepan. Heat over medium heat, stirring until the sugar dissolves. Allow it to cool before using.

Infuse Mint:
- In a small bowl, muddle the fresh mint leaves to release their flavor. You can also gently bruise them with the back of a spoon.

Prepare Eucalyptus Oil or Syrup:
- If using eucalyptus oil, ensure it is food-grade and only use a drop or two. Alternatively, you can make eucalyptus syrup by combining water, sugar, and a few eucalyptus leaves in a saucepan. Heat until the sugar dissolves, then strain.

Combine Lemon Juice, Sweetener, and Infusions:
- In a large pitcher, combine the fresh lemon juice, honey or simple syrup, muddled mint leaves, and eucalyptus oil or syrup. Stir well to combine.

Add Cold Water:
- Pour the cold water into the pitcher and mix thoroughly. Taste and adjust sweetness or eucalyptus flavor as needed.

Chill:
- Refrigerate the lemonade for at least 1-2 hours to allow the flavors to meld.

Strain (Optional):

- If you prefer a smoother lemonade, you can strain the mixture to remove the mint leaves before serving.

Serve over Ice:
- Fill glasses with ice cubes and pour the Eucalyptus and Mint Lemonade over the ice.

Garnish:
- Garnish each glass with a slice of lemon and a sprig of fresh mint.

Stir Before Serving:
- Give the lemonade a gentle stir before serving to distribute the mint and eucalyptus flavors.

Enjoy:
- Sip and enjoy the refreshing and invigorating taste of Eucalyptus and Mint Lemonade!

Kangaroo Island Gin and Tonic

Ingredients:

- 2 oz (60 ml) Kangaroo Island Gin
- Tonic water
- Ice cubes
- Fresh lime slices or wedges, for garnish
- Fresh juniper berries (optional, for garnish)

Instructions:

Chill Glass:
- Place a glass in the freezer for a few minutes to chill.

Add Ice Cubes:
- Once the glass is chilled, fill it with ice cubes.

Pour Kangaroo Island Gin:
- Measure 2 ounces (60 ml) of Kangaroo Island Gin and pour it over the ice in the glass.

Top with Tonic Water:
- Top up the glass with tonic water. Adjust the ratio of gin to tonic according to your preference.

Gentle Stir:
- Give the mixture a gentle stir to combine the gin and tonic.

Garnish:
- Garnish the Kangaroo Island Gin and Tonic with fresh lime slices or wedges. For an extra touch, you can add a few fresh juniper berries.

Serve Immediately:
- Serve the Kangaroo Island Gin and Tonic immediately while it's cold and refreshing.

Enjoy Responsibly:
- Sip and enjoy the unique flavors of Kangaroo Island Gin in this classic and iconic cocktail. Remember to drink responsibly.

Bush Tucker Mojito

Ingredients:

- 2 oz (60 ml) white rum
- 1 oz (30 ml) lemon myrtle and lime juice (combined)
- 1 oz (30 ml) simple syrup
- 8-10 fresh mint leaves
- Soda water
- Ice cubes
- Lime slices and mint sprigs for garnish

Instructions:

Prepare Lemon Myrtle and Lime Juice:
- Combine lemon myrtle leaves with freshly squeezed lime juice. Allow them to infuse for about 10-15 minutes, then strain to extract the flavored juice.

Muddle Mint Leaves:
- In a glass, muddle the fresh mint leaves to release their flavor. Be gentle to avoid tearing the leaves.

Add Simple Syrup:
- Pour the simple syrup over the muddled mint leaves.

Add Lemon Myrtle and Lime Juice:
- Add the lemon myrtle and lime juice to the glass.

Pour White Rum:
- Measure 2 ounces (60 ml) of white rum and add it to the glass.

Fill with Ice Cubes:
- Fill the glass with ice cubes.

Stir Gently:
- Stir the ingredients gently to combine and chill the mixture.

Top with Soda Water:
- Top up the glass with soda water. Adjust the amount according to your preference for sweetness and effervescence.

Garnish:
- Garnish the Bush Tucker Mojito with lime slices and a sprig of fresh mint.

Serve Immediately:
- Serve the Bush Tucker Mojito immediately while it's cold and effervescent.

Enjoy Responsibly:
- Sip and enjoy the refreshing flavors of this unique Bush Tucker Mojito. Remember to drink responsibly.

Golden Gaytime Cocktail

Ingredients:

- 1 1/2 oz (45 ml) butterscotch schnapps
- 1 oz (30 ml) crème de cacao
- 1 oz (30 ml) Baileys Irish Cream
- 1 oz (30 ml) vanilla vodka
- 1 oz (30 ml) milk or cream
- Crushed honeycomb or caramel for rimming (optional)
- Ice cubes

Instructions:

Prepare Glass:
- If desired, rim the glass with crushed honeycomb or caramel by dipping the rim in honey or simple syrup, then into the crushed topping.

Fill Shaker with Ice:
- Fill a cocktail shaker with ice cubes.

Add Butterscotch Schnapps:
- Pour 1 1/2 ounces (45 ml) of butterscotch schnapps into the shaker.

Add Crème de Cacao:
- Add 1 ounce (30 ml) of crème de cacao to the shaker.

Add Baileys Irish Cream:
- Pour in 1 ounce (30 ml) of Baileys Irish Cream.

Add Vanilla Vodka:
- Add 1 ounce (30 ml) of vanilla vodka to the mix.

Add Milk or Cream:
- Pour in 1 ounce (30 ml) of milk or cream.

Shake Well:
- Secure the lid on the shaker and shake the ingredients well to chill the mixture.

Strain into Glass:
- Strain the cocktail into your prepared glass.

Serve on the Rocks:
- You can serve the Golden Gaytime Cocktail over ice if desired.

Garnish (Optional):
- Garnish the cocktail with a sprinkle of crushed honeycomb or caramel on top.

Enjoy:

- Sip and enjoy the indulgent and sweet flavors of the Golden Gaytime Cocktail. Cheers!

Baking and Sweet Treats:

Vanilla Slice

Ingredients:

For the Custard Filling:

- 2 cups whole milk
- 1 cup heavy cream
- 1 cup granulated sugar
- 1/2 cup cornstarch
- 4 large egg yolks
- 1 teaspoon vanilla extract

For the Pastry Layers:

- 2 sheets puff pastry, thawed
- Icing sugar for dusting

Instructions:

For the Custard Filling:

> Prepare Baking Dish:
> - Line a square baking dish with parchment paper, leaving an overhang on the sides for easy removal.
>
> Combine Milk and Cream:
> - In a saucepan, combine the whole milk and heavy cream. Heat over medium heat until it just begins to simmer. Do not boil.
>
> Whisk Sugar and Cornstarch:
> - In a bowl, whisk together the granulated sugar and cornstarch.
>
> Add Egg Yolks:
> - Add the egg yolks to the sugar and cornstarch mixture, whisking until well combined.
>
> Temper Eggs:
> - Slowly pour the hot milk and cream mixture into the egg mixture, whisking constantly to temper the eggs.
>
> Return to Heat:

- Pour the combined mixture back into the saucepan and return to the stove. Cook over medium heat, stirring constantly until the custard thickens.

Add Vanilla Extract:
- Once thickened, remove from heat and stir in the vanilla extract. Allow the custard to cool slightly.

For the Pastry Layers:

Bake Puff Pastry:
- Preheat your oven according to the puff pastry package instructions. Roll out the puff pastry sheets to fit your baking dish. Bake the puff pastry according to package instructions until golden brown and puffed.

Layer Pastry and Custard:
- Place one sheet of baked puff pastry in the bottom of the prepared baking dish. Pour the slightly cooled custard over the pastry, spreading it evenly.

Top with Second Pastry Sheet:
- Place the second sheet of baked puff pastry on top of the custard layer.

Chill:
- Allow the vanilla slice to cool in the refrigerator for at least 4 hours or overnight to set.

Dust with Icing Sugar:
- Before serving, dust the top of the vanilla slice with icing sugar.

Slice and Serve:
- Lift the vanilla slice from the baking dish using the parchment paper overhang. Slice into squares and serve.

Enjoy:
- Enjoy this classic Vanilla Slice with its layers of flaky puff pastry and creamy custard filling!

Passionfruit Sponge Cake

Ingredients:

For the Sponge Cake:

- 4 large eggs
- 1 cup granulated sugar
- 1 cup all-purpose flour
- 1 teaspoon baking powder
- Pinch of salt

For the Passionfruit Filling:

- 1 cup fresh passionfruit pulp (about 8-10 passionfruits)
- 1/2 cup granulated sugar
- 1 tablespoon cornstarch
- 1 tablespoon water

For the Whipped Cream:

- 1 cup heavy cream
- 2 tablespoons powdered sugar
- 1 teaspoon vanilla extract

Additional:

- Fresh passionfruit seeds for garnish (optional)

Instructions:

For the Sponge Cake:

Preheat Oven:
- Preheat your oven to 350°F (175°C). Grease and line two 8-inch round cake pans with parchment paper.

Prepare Dry Ingredients:
- In a bowl, sift together the all-purpose flour, baking powder, and a pinch of salt. Set aside.

Whip Eggs and Sugar:

- In a large mixing bowl, beat the eggs and granulated sugar together until the mixture becomes thick, pale, and triples in volume. This may take about 5-7 minutes with an electric mixer.

Fold in Dry Ingredients:
- Gently fold the sifted dry ingredients into the egg and sugar mixture using a spatula, being careful not to deflate the batter.

Divide and Bake:
- Divide the batter evenly between the prepared cake pans. Smooth the tops with a spatula. Bake in the preheated oven for 20-25 minutes or until a toothpick inserted into the center comes out clean.

Cool:
- Allow the sponge cakes to cool in the pans for 10 minutes, then transfer them to a wire rack to cool completely.

For the Passionfruit Filling:

Prepare Passionfruit Pulp:
- Cut the passionfruits in half and scoop out the pulp into a bowl.

Cook Passionfruit Filling:
- In a saucepan, combine the passionfruit pulp and granulated sugar. Bring to a simmer over medium heat.

Make Cornstarch Slurry:
- In a small bowl, mix the cornstarch with water to create a slurry.

Thicken Filling:
- Add the cornstarch slurry to the simmering passionfruit mixture, stirring constantly until it thickens. Remove from heat and let it cool.

For the Whipped Cream:

Whip Heavy Cream:
- In a separate bowl, whip the heavy cream, powdered sugar, and vanilla extract until stiff peaks form.

Assemble the Cake:

Layer Sponge Cake and Filling:
- Place one of the sponge cakes on a serving plate. Spread a layer of the passionfruit filling over the cake.

Add Whipped Cream:
- Spoon a layer of whipped cream over the passionfruit filling.

Top with Second Cake Layer:

- Place the second sponge cake layer on top.

Frost with Whipped Cream:
- Frost the top and sides of the cake with the remaining whipped cream.

Garnish (Optional):
- Garnish the cake with fresh passionfruit seeds if desired.

Chill:
- Refrigerate the Passionfruit Sponge Cake for at least 1-2 hours before serving to allow the flavors to meld.

Slice and Serve:
- Slice and serve this delightful Passionfruit Sponge Cake. Enjoy the light sponge, tangy passionfruit filling, and billowy whipped cream!

Milo Cheesecake

Ingredients:

For the Crust:

- 2 cups chocolate cookie crumbs
- 1/2 cup unsalted butter, melted

For the Cheesecake Filling:

- 24 oz (680g) cream cheese, softened
- 1 cup granulated sugar
- 3/4 cup Milo powder
- 4 large eggs
- 1 teaspoon vanilla extract
- 1/2 cup sour cream

For the Topping:

- 1 cup whipped cream
- Additional Milo powder for dusting

Instructions:

For the Crust:

Preheat Oven:
- Preheat your oven to 325°F (160°C). Grease a 9-inch springform pan.

Combine Crumbs and Butter:
- In a bowl, mix the chocolate cookie crumbs and melted butter until well combined.

Press into Pan:
- Press the mixture into the bottom of the prepared springform pan to create an even crust.

Bake:
- Bake the crust in the preheated oven for about 10 minutes. Remove and let it cool while you prepare the cheesecake filling.

For the Cheesecake Filling:

Reduce Oven Temperature:

- Reduce the oven temperature to 300°F (150°C).

Prepare Cream Cheese Mixture:
- In a large bowl, beat the softened cream cheese until smooth. Add sugar and Milo powder, continuing to beat until well combined.

Add Eggs:
- Add the eggs one at a time, mixing well after each addition.

Incorporate Vanilla and Sour Cream:
- Mix in the vanilla extract and sour cream until the mixture is smooth.

Pour into Crust:
- Pour the cream cheese mixture over the prepared crust in the springform pan.

Bake:
- Bake in the preheated oven for about 50-60 minutes or until the center is set. The edges should be slightly golden.

Cool and Chill:
- Allow the cheesecake to cool in the pan, then refrigerate for several hours or overnight.

For the Topping:

Whip Cream:
- Whip the cream until stiff peaks form.

Top Cheesecake:
- Spread the whipped cream over the chilled cheesecake.

Dust with Milo:
- Dust the top of the cheesecake with additional Milo powder.

Slice and Serve:
- Slice and serve this decadent Milo Cheesecake. Enjoy the rich chocolatey flavor and creamy texture!

Note:
- You can also drizzle chocolate syrup or ganache over the top for an extra chocolatey touch if desired.

www.ingramcontent.com/pod-product-compliance
Lightning Source LLC
LaVergne TN
LVHW081555060526
838201LV00054B/1898